MASTER YOUR THINKING

A PRACTICAL GUIDE TO ALIGN YOURSELF
WITH REALITY AND ACHIEVE TANGIBLE
RESULTS IN THE REAL WORLD

THIBAUT MEURISSE

Why this book

Over the years, I've encountered a lot of people who have a flawed model of reality. They would tell me their goals and how excited they were to achieve them; however, when looking at their approach, I could clearly see they lacked a proper understanding of what was required to achieve those goals. This would manifest in different ways, such as:

- A level of action out of alignment with their ambitious goals (i.e. insufficient action),
- A poor strategy,
- A blind conviction they were on the right track, even when they were not, and/or
- An unwillingness to listen to feedback and reconsider their approach.

There is nothing wrong with pursuing ambitious visions. I have a crazy vision myself and I believe in the importance of having inspiring life visions. The problem arises when people spend months or even years acting in a way that rarely allows them to move closer to their vision—often unknowingly.

That's why I wrote this book. This book will help you think more accurately, and it will help you design and enact an effective strategy to increase your odds of achieving your goals. Life is too short for you to waste time doing things that fail to bring the results you want.

Who is this book for

You'll greatly benefit from this book if you recognize yourself in one or more of the following situations:

- You've been pursuing a specific goal for months or years but have failed to make significant progress.
- You want to assess your chances of success for any future endeavors.
- You want to develop highly effective strategies to help you achieve your goals.
- You want to achieve any future goals or dreams faster than you normally would.

If any of the above points resonate with you, read on.

INTRODUCTION

Do you have big dreams but don't seem to make progress toward them? Do you wonder whether you should even try to chase these dreams? Perhaps you think you are deluding yourself?

We live in a world where doing certain things will get you positive results, while doing others will not. This is the law of cause and effect. Therefore, one of the most important skills you can develop is the ability to create an accurate model of reality. In other words, you need to develop the ability to understand how reality works to help you act in a way that is more likely to produce the results you want.

Unfortunately, this isn't as simple as it may appear. This is especially true in today's world, where the influx of information we receive can be overwhelming. But developing an accurate model of reality is vital. People who are serious about achieving their goals continuously seek to develop a better model of reality. These individuals are obsessed with finding out what works while, at the same time, letting go of what doesn't.

On the other hand, mediocre or unsuccessful people tend to rely on flawed models of reality. Because they fail to grasp how reality works, they are unable to create an effective blueprint to achieve their goals. This leads them to try all sorts of things and, when none of the gimmicks or tactics they use work, they end up feeling discouraged.

Throughout this book, we will discover that the better you understand reality, the better armed you will be to take the actions needed to achieve the results you want. As you learn to build more effective models of reality, you will be able to skyrocket results in all areas of your life.

In *Part I. Letting go of inaccurate thinking*, you'll discover the common errors in thinking people make, and learn how to think more accurately. Furthermore, as you develop more accurate thinking, you'll be able to take effective action which, in turn, will help you achieve tangible results.

In *Part II. Aligning yourself with reality*, we'll discuss the importance of being in alignment with reality and see how you can move toward this position. Among other things, you'll learn how to make better assumptions, gather information more effectively and ask smarter questions. As you further align yourself with reality, you'll be able to create better strategies and implement effective processes that will bring you the results you want.

Finally, in *Part III. Empowering your model of reality*, we'll see how to make your model of reality work for you. You'll learn how to design an empowering environment, develop rock-solid confidence and expand your field of possibilities. And by doing this, you will increase your odds of achieving any goal you set your mind to.

So, are you ready to align with reality and achieve tangible results in the real world? If so, read on.

YOUR FREE STEP-BY-STEP ACTION GUIDE

To help you develop accurate thinking, I've created a free action guide. Make sure you download it at the following URL:

http://whatispersonaldevelopment.org/myt-workbook

If you have any difficulty downloading the action guide, contact me at:

thibaut.meurisse@gmail.com

I will send you a copy as soon as possible.

Alternatively, you can use the action guide available at the end of this book.

PART I

LETTING GO OF
INACCURATE THINKING

Are you thinking straight?

Chances are, you're not.

The truth is, it's almost impossible to develop a completely accurate picture of the world or any part of it. There are just too many variables and too much conflicting information out there. Not to mention the variety of biases we're subject to or the countless tricks our mind plays on us.

The point is, thinking well is challenging. However, it is our responsibility to sharpen our thinking so we can develop an accurate model of reality. This, in turn, will help us take effective action and make a difference in the world around us.

Please note, in this book, we will define "model of reality" as the sum of all the beliefs we hold. This includes our political beliefs, our religious beliefs, as well as the beliefs we have about ourselves, our lives, or our work, to name just a few factors. The more accurate our beliefs can be, the better decisions we can make—

and the better the results we will achieve. This is why accurate thinking is absolutely critical to our success.

In this section, we'll spend some time investigating all the ways your current thinking might be inaccurate. We'll look at the common mistakes you make in terms of your thought processes, your "thinking", we'll explore how your beliefs are created and we'll see how your emotions can trick you. As you learn to let go of inaccurate thinking, you'll develop a better model of reality, leading you to achieve better results.

In this book, we'll define inaccurate thinking as thinking in a biased way, which includes:

- Holding onto wrong assumptions that don't reflect reality,
- Falling for cognitive biases that cloud your judgment,
- Being a victim of common disempowering thought patterns, or
- Letting your emotional state influence your decisions.

But before we go into each of the above points in more detail, let's review some of the consequences of thinking inaccurately.

1

THE COST OF INACCURATE THINKING

Because your thought processes determine the actions you take, thinking inaccurately can have negative consequences. It can lead you to make poor decisions that may prevent you from achieving optimal results. For instance, among other things, inaccurate thinking can:

- Create unnecessary suffering in your life,
- Lead you to waste a lot of time and energy,
- Make you feel bad, and
- Lead you to feel overwhelmed.

A. Inaccurate thinking creates unnecessary suffering in your life

Inaccurate thinking can be the source of countless dramas and can create more suffering than needed in your life.

In this situation, you fall prey to various biases or make snap judgments. For example, the poor assumptions you're making might lead you to misinterpret what someone said or did. In fact, many issues, such as miscommunication, are the result of poor thinking skills and misinterpretation.

Let me give you one example. One of my friends wanted to create a Meetup event to help people connect more intimately through various games. He contacted a woman who organizes international parties on Meetup for advice. When she failed to reply to his message, my friend wondered whether she perceived him as a competitor.

I advised him to be extra careful when making such contentious assumptions and suggested there could be many reasons why she didn't reply to his message. She might have had personal or professional issues. She may have missed his message. Or she may simply have forgotten. As it turned out, she had been sick. Eventually, she did reply, which showed she had no misgivings regarding his approach.

The lesson here is that, in the absence of specific data or clear information to verify your assumptions, you should avoid making them at all. However, if you *are* to assume anything, try to come up with the most positive assumption you can think of. Also, whenever possible, take the necessary steps to verify any and all assumptions. For instance:

- Rather than assuming someone doesn't like your idea because they seem distracted during your presentation, ask them directly. Don't resent them or create a whole story in your mind without verifying your supposition.
- Rather than assuming a person doesn't like you, check until you're sure that's the case beyond any reasonable doubt.

The bottom line is, avoid making negative assumptions. Instead, take action and search for the truth. By doing so, you'll get rid of many potentially negative issues in your life.

Action step

Using your action guide, write down two or three examples of inaccurate assumptions you may be making right now or have made in the past.

B. Inaccurate thinking leads you to waste time

Have you ever spent a lot of time doing something that didn't need to be done in the first place?

People who fail to take enough time to think things through can easily fall into this trap. Inaccurate or insufficient thinking may lead you to:

1. Work on low-value tasks, or
2. Approach tasks in the wrong way.

1. Working on low-value tasks

Time is one of your most precious assets. Every second you waste is lost forever. If you don't think before you act, you risk wasting time working on the wrong things. Are you certain the task you're about to begin is really that important, or would you be better off tackling a more important one?

In truth, only a few of the actions you take will generate most of your results. The rest will barely move the needle forward. Consequently, your job is to identify the key activities to focus your time and energy on. This concept is often referred to as the "80/20 Principle". According to this principle, twenty percent of your actions will generate eighty percent of your results. Therefore, you should identify your twenty percent and focus on it while delegating or removing the remaining ineffective eighty percent. Of course, this is not an exact science. It is possible that ten percent of your actions will lead to ninety percent of your successful results. Or perhaps just one percent of your tasks will generate fifty percent or more of your overall output.

The point is, thinking accurately involves identifying your key tasks and focusing most of your efforts on those.

Bonus tip: Your key tasks tend to be the ones you want to do the least and/or those tasks that consume the most of your energy.

In *Part II. Aligning yourself with reality*, we'll see how you can create an effective strategy to ensure you work on the right tasks and approach them in the correct way.

2. Approaching tasks the wrong way

Now, working on your key tasks is not enough. You must also ensure you approach them the right way. To do so, before beginning any new task, ask yourself what you can do to complete it as quickly and as effectively as possible. For instance:

- Could you re-use or modify an existing template?
- Could you ask an experienced friend for advice?
- Could you break down the task even further?

Taking a few minutes to think before diving headfirst into a challenge can often save you a lot of time and headaches. Personally, before starting a task or project, I like to ask myself one simple, yet fundamental question: Who can help me? In other words, who knows the answers to my questions or understands the blueprint to follow to help me achieve my goal?

The truth is, most of the things you're trying to achieve have already been achieved by other people before you. Therefore, why reinvent the wheel? Why go through the hassle of figuring out things by yourself when you could ask others?

Now, let me give you a couple of examples from my personal life.

Example 1: Last year, a Russian publisher offered to buy the foreign rights of one of my books. Because I had never sold my foreign rights before, I wasn't sure how to proceed. So, I contacted an author who I knew sold the foreign rights of his books. I asked him if he would be willing to look into the contract I received from the publisher, which he kindly agreed to do. Not only did he give me the help I needed, we became friends, too. I call that a win-win!

Example 2: One of my goals this year is to have three of my books translated into Spanish, French and German. Knowing it would take me hours to find the right translators, I kept procrastinating on that goal.

Then I remembered that one of my author friends had already translated his book into foreign languages. So I asked him how he found his translators. He kindly introduced me to his Spanish, French and German translators and proofreaders which saved me a great deal of time and energy.

Don't get me wrong, though. I'm not saying you should "use" other people for your own benefit. I always try to help people as much as I can, and I believe you should, too. But why not ask others to share with you what they already know while you reciprocate for them? You'll save each other a lot of time and frustration.

Below are additional questions to help you approach a task with maximum effectiveness:

- Who do I know who has already achieved my goal?
- Do I know anyone able to put me in contact with someone who has achieved my goal?
- Who could tell me the best blueprint to reach my goal?
- Who could give me the most valuable advice (based on personal experience, not just theory)?

- Who could tell me where to look for the right information?

* * *

Action step

Look at everything you did this week. Were these tasks all absolutely essential? Were any unnecessary? Write down your answer in your action guide.

C. Inaccurate thinking leads you to feel bad about yourself

You now understand that thinking inaccurately can lead you to take ineffective actions which can prevent you from achieving your goals. Another side-effect is that, as you keep failing to reach your targets, you begin to lose confidence in yourself. You may start believing that something is wrong with you, that perhaps you're just "not good enough". However, the real issue is usually your lack of understanding of the way reality works. Put differently, you may have built poor models of reality by failing to:

- Gather adequate information,
- Gain sufficient experience, or
- Cultivate accurate thinking.

For instance, you may believe that just by buying a course and completing all the exercises, you'll be able to find enough clients to become a full-time coach within three months and finally quit your soul-crushing job. However, this thinking is likely to be unrealistic. You may have failed to take some components into consideration. As you embark upon your task, you may discover that it takes more time and effort than you originally imagined. In which case, you may feel discouraged and give up.

By learning to think more accurately and realistically, you'll start feeling better about yourself. You'll realize you're doing okay, and you will set more realistic goals. Doing so will enable you to accumulate small wins and boost your confidence over time.

For example, instead of hoping to be coaching full-time within three months, you could give yourself two years to grow your coaching business, celebrating each milestone along the way (e.g., your first client, your first $1,000 month, et cetera).

Bonus tip: To avoid feeling bad or discouraged, see beyond the success stories used by marketers. Yes, some people do become wildly successful within a few months—but these people are in a tiny minority. They are unicorns whose success could be explained by a variety of factors such as previous experience, rare personality traits or luck. Most people will need to put in a lot of time and effort before they can achieve concrete results. Some of the most successful people on earth spent years working on their craft before they could become "overnight successes". So, be patient. Keep going.

Action step

Using your action guide, write down three situations when you had unrealistic expectations and felt disappointed or frustrated when you failed to achieve your goals or reach your targets. Then write down your answer to the following questions:

- What is one current goal for which you may have unrealistic expectations?
- How could you adjust your expectations to make them more realistic?

D. Inaccurate thinking leads you to feel overwhelmed

By failing to take the time to think, it is easy to become swamped by the sea of information available. Thinking accurately means being able to sort through the information, separating the relevant from the irrelevant. Relevant information includes everything you need to know now to achieve your goals. Irrelevant information encompasses everything else. Of course, it doesn't mean you should consume only information you'll use right away, but it does mean you should avoid consuming more information than you need.

Most of the information we consume today is noise which is not only unnecessary, but also counterproductive. Keeping up to date with new tactics, tricks and other gimmicks will only lead you to jump from one thing to the next, never getting any closer to your goals. Realize that most of the principles you need to apply to reach your goals remain constant. They do not change every day. They will often work for years and years. Consequently, trying different tactics on a whim is unlikely to lead to sudden success. What you need is a sound strategy.

In other words, the less you get caught up in the incessant flow of data, the better you'll be able to separate noise from valuable information. This will make it easier for you to look at the bigger picture and craft an effective strategy that will work for you.

In the third book in this series, *Master Your Focus*, I explain in detail how to select the necessary information, while eliminating everything else, to help you develop laser-sharp focus and achieve tangible results.

* * *

Action step

Fill in the table in your action guide. To do so:

- In the first column, write down all the information you consumed in the past seven days (e.g., books, articles or emails you read, websites, videos, et cetera).
- In the second column, write down "U" for useful information or "N" for noise.
- In the third column, write down the concrete actions you will take do deal with information you've identified as noise.

To conclude, inaccurate thinking comes at a high price. When you fail to think clearly, you'll make many poor decisions which will cost you time and money. So make sure you avoid:

- Making negative assumptions without checking whether they are accurate,
- Starting a task without thinking things through beforehand,
- Substituting thinking for hard work,
- Having unrealistic expectations, and
- Consuming too much irrelevant information.

Now, let's look in more detail at some of the reasons your current thinking may be inaccurate.

WHY YOUR CURRENT THINKING IS INACCURATE

It's impossible to have a completely accurate vision of the world. We all fall prey to biases and tend to rely on snap judgments to make decisions. Fortunately, there are tools we can use to develop our ability to think more accurately and make better decisions.

Let's review a few reasons why your thinking may be inaccurate and see what you can do about it.

A. Poor assumptions distort your thinking

Your thinking might be inaccurate because you made, or are making, bad assumptions that poorly reflect the reality around you.

The truth is, you make assumptions all day long. Many of these assumptions have little impact on your life, but some can have severe repercussions. As we've seen before, what you believe dictates how you think, feel and act. Therefore, having incorrect assumptions (i.e., thinking inaccurately) will lead you to take wrong actions and achieve poor results. For this reason, you must learn to challenge your assumptions. Whenever I coach a client or interact with someone, I try to identify each negative assumption they may have. Some of which could be:

- You can't have it all, right?
- I can't make money doing this.
- I'm not smart enough.
- I need to work harder.

But are these statements accurate? They may or may not be.

What about you? What major assumptions are you making in your life? Each inaccurate assumption you hold onto creates limitations. The moment you believe something is impossible, it will almost never become your reality. For this reason, you must be extra careful when you make assumptions: they have real consequences in the real world.

For instance, let's assume you believe that the sole purpose of your job is to pay the bills. If so, what are the odds you end up designing your dream career?

I remember a conversation I had with my supervisor when working in Japan years ago. He told me that I didn't need to like my job, that I should just collect my paycheck and enjoy my free time. Perhaps he was right. Maybe a job only serves to pay the bills. But it didn't seem quite right to me at the time. I couldn't resign myself to spending the rest of my life jumping from one unfulfilling job to the next just to make ends meet.

If I had bought into my boss' idea, I would probably never have built a career I'm passionate about. This demonstrates how dangerous assumptions can be. Holding just one erroneous assumption can limit your possibilities and destroy your potential for growth and fulfillment.

Let's have a look at one more example.

Imagine one of your assumptions is that money is evil. If so, what are the chances you end up wealthy? Very slim. Why would you want to be associated with anything evil?

I hope by now you understand how limiting erroneous assumptions can be. What you believe will often become your reality. So be careful what you wish for.

Now does this mean that assumptions are useless? No. They exist for a reason. Let's see *why* we make assumptions.

* * *

Action step

Using your action guide, write down three disempowering assumptions you may be making in your life right now.

1. Why we make assumptions

Our brains need to give meaning to things and events as an attempt to understand them. This is why we can't help but interpret everything that happens to us. For instance, some of our ancestors saw natural disasters as a manifestation of Gods' wrath and chose to perform rituals to appease these deities.

Similarly, your assumptions provide you with a framework you can use to navigate through life and make decisions. You may hold assumptions about the nature of work, the meaning of life or the way politics works. The more accurate these are, the better decisions you'll make—and the better results you will be able to achieve.

Please note, making assumptions is inevitable. Your mind automatically processes the information around you and interprets it, thereby creating a model of reality that is unique to you. Without assumptions, you have no criteria you can use to assess whether an action is relevant which would prevent you from making any sound decision.

In my book, *Crush Your Limits*, I reveal fifty assumptions that may be preventing you from living the life you want. You can learn more.

2. Where your assumptions come from

As detailed above, our minds generate assumptions. But have you ever wondered where these assumptions come from? Why do you hold onto some assumptions while your neighbor holds onto others? Your assumptions are part of the model of reality you've built throughout your life. To understand where they come from, we need to look in more detail at how you created your model of reality.

3. How your model of reality is created.

Your model of reality encompasses all the assumptions (or beliefs) you rely on to give meaning to the world around you. Each of us has our own subjective model of reality, which may be more or less accurate. The beliefs that constitute your model of reality come from different sources such as:

- Your parents,
- Your teachers,
- The media (newspaper, TV, internet et cetera),
- Your friends and peers,
- Your own experiences, and
- Your interpretation.

Let's go through each one.

a. Your parents

Your parents play an important part in shaping your model of reality. They do so by passing their beliefs onto you. Note that sometimes, instead of adopting your parents' beliefs, you take the opposite beliefs, whether consciously or unconsciously. For instance:

- Witnessing your parents' penny-pinching may lead you to spend your money frivolously or even fall into debt.
- Having strict parents may lead you to become more lenient with your own children.

In short, you tend to mimic your parents or do the exact opposite. Now, it's up to you to look closer at the beliefs you inherited and change them as and when necessary.

b. Your teachers

School also influences your model of reality through the interaction you have with your teachers and classmates. No matter how neutral your teachers intend to be, they have their own vision of the world. The beliefs transmitted to you during your school years will depend on a variety of factors, such as the type of school you attended, your teachers and classmates or the country you lived in, among other factors.

In short, school isn't neutral. It influences your beliefs and shapes your ongoing model of reality.

c. The media

Media also has a huge influence. TV channels, newspapers and other media outlets have their own agenda and biases. For instance, they tend to report negative events such as riots, crimes or natural disasters while ignoring positive news. Why? Because bad news sells. This can lead you to believe the world is a worse place than it actually is.

Try completing the following sentence:

In the last twenty years, the proportion of the world population living in extreme poverty has ...

A: Almost doubled.

B: Remained more or less the same.

C: Almost halved.

The correct answer is C: almost halved.

Did you get it right? Only four percent of French, five percent of American and nine percent of British people did. This information was taken from Hans Rosling's book, *Factfulness*. In his book, Rosling demonstrates that, contrary to what many of us believe, in many aspects things are improving the world over.

The point is, what's reported on the news isn't truly representative of the actual state of the world. Now, why does this matter? Because misinterpreting reality comes with real-world consequences. For instance, believing the world is worse than it is may lead you to lose hope. As a result, you may not bother taking any action to improve it. Your inaccurate perception of the world may also lead you to waste a lot of time and effort addressing the wrong problems while ignoring more urgent issues. This is the cost of having an inaccurate model of reality. It's not just theory.

d. Your friends and peers

Your friends, colleagues and peers will inevitably influence your perception of the world. If you're not careful, pessimistic people will kill your dreams. On the other hand, positive people will inspire you, increasing the odds you'll accomplish great things, sometimes far beyond anything you can imagine.

To learn how to surround yourself with positive people and design a more empowering environment, refer to the section, *Designing an empowering environment* in Part III of this book.

e. Your own experiences

Everything you experience, whether positive or negative, is feedback from reality. In other words, as you take action in the real world, you receive valuable information from the reality around you. The feedback you receive may confirm what you previously thought, or it may refute it, forcing you to revise your original model.

For instance, you may believe you did an excellent job with your homework only to receive a bad grade from your teacher. This feedback from reality will force you to revise your stance and take the necessary action to improve your performance (e.g., take extra classes, ask your friends for help, et cetera).

The more action you take, the more feedback you receive, and the more opportunities you have to make better assumptions and refine your model of reality.

f. Your interpretation

Experience is a great teacher. However, what shapes your model of reality isn't only what you experience, but also the way you interpret it. And the way you interpret your experiences is based on the assumptions you hold. By learning to make better assumptions, you'll give more constructive meaning to your experiences. This, in turn, will lead you to take smarter actions and produce better results.

For example, if you assume every setback you face moves you closer to your goals, you'll be more inclined to learn from your mistakes rather than be disheartened by them. However, if you see setbacks as a sign that you're not capable enough, you'll likely avoid making mistakes which will hamper your growth. Similarly, if you assume people have good intentions, you'll interpret situations more positively than if you believe these same people want to take advantage of you.

Now that we've seen how your assumptions are made and how they contribute to creating your model of reality, let's have a look at common biases that further distort your thinking.

* * *

Action step

Using your action guide, write down one limiting assumption you may have adopted from each of the sources below:

- Your parents and family.
- Your teachers.
- Your friends and peers.
- The media.
- Your experiences.
- Your interpretation.

B. Five common biases that distort your thinking

As human beings, we're prone to fall prey to a variety of biases. This is just how our brain works. To become a better thinker, you must become acutely aware of the major biases you may be the victim of.

Now it's not possible to be completely unbiased. To do so, you would have to be aware of your thoughts 24/7 which would demand far more energy than you have. However, during key moments that require you to make sound decisions, you can make yourself more aware of your biggest biases.

In this section, we'll review some of the major biases that may lead you to think inaccurately. We'll see how you can overcome these biases and sharpen your thinking to place you in a better position to achieve your goals. The biases we will cover are:

1. The self-serving bias,
2. The sunk cost fallacy,
3. The planning fallacy,
4. The survivorship bias, and
5. The Dunning-Kruger Effect.

1. Self-serving bias

This is when you attribute your successes to your skills, but attribute your failures to bad luck. This bias leads you to obsess over the outcome while paying scant attention to the process. When the outcome is favorable, you assume the process is right (although it may not be). When the outcome is unfavorable, you call yourself unlucky, even though you may have followed the correct process.

We have to admit that luck plays a role in many situations, especially in the short term. Therefore, merely looking at the immediate outcome can be misleading. Instead, you must pay close attention to the process and keep refining it by analyzing case studies, experimenting and learning from feedback. You must strive to identify the correct actions. By taking the right actions repeatedly, you'll increase the chances of striking it "lucky" at some point.

How to deal with self-serving bias

To avoid being a victim of this bias:

- Put emphasis on the process. Focus on what you need to do every day to maximize your chances of achieving your long-term goals.
- Avoid assuming your process is effective just because you obtained good short-term results. Instead, keep working on refining it over time.
- Never assume you know it all. Stay open-minded and

listen to the feedback you receive from the people around you.

2. The sunk cost fallacy

To think accurately, you must assess the actions you're taking today based on their sole ability to get you where you want to be. Too often, people fall for what is called the "sunk cost fallacy". That is, they make decisions based on their past actions rather than on the present. They let the time, money and energy they've spent in the past influence their decisions. However, from a logical point of view, everything they did in the past is largely irrelevant. Here are some examples of how the sunk cost fallacy works.

- Having spent months or years working on your business, you decide to keep going even though you should probably give up and move on to another venture.
- Having spent hundreds of dollars on your book cover, you refuse to change it even though it's hindering your sales.
- Having been in a relationship for years, you refuse to move out of it even though it might be best for you both in the long term.

In all the examples above, you choose to maintain the status quo because of a variety of factors from the past while ignoring what your present self really wants. By doing so, you neglect your present self and act against the interests of the future self you want to become.

To guard yourself against the sunk cost fallacy, you can practice what is called "zero-based thinking". To do so, ask yourself the following question:

Knowing what I now know, would I still ... today?

For example:

- Knowing what I now know, would I still *start that business* today?
- Knowing what I now know, would I still *take that job* today?
- Knowing what I now know, would I still *buy that book cover* today?
- Knowing what I now know, would I still *start that relationship* today?

If your answer is no, it indicates your present self wants something else.

Another way to overcome sunk cost fallacy is to learn to value your future self more highly. There is no need to please your past self anymore, but your future self is counting on you to make the best decisions today to maximize your happiness tomorrow. Ask yourself this question:

If you were your future self five years from now, what would you want your present self to do for you today?

3. Planning fallacy

We're terrible at planning. When we think of something we'd like to achieve, we fail to consider all the things that could go wrong. This is why many projects are delayed and/or end up costing far more than originally planned.

Thinking accurately entails making better forecasts to help you create more realistic plans. When you hold onto unrealistic expectations, you might feel demotivated when things don't turn out as planned. You may even believe that you aren't smart enough and that something is wrong with you. By failing to deliver on what you promised, you may also get into trouble with your customers.

How to overcome planning fallacy

One of the best ways to avoid falling prey to the planning fallacy is to get into the habit of giving yourself more time to complete your tasks or projects. A good idea is to double the time you think you'll need to finish a given project.

For long-term projects, ask yourself what could go wrong. Look at similar projects you've completed in the past and see what problems you encountered and how much time and effort it took to solve them. Alternatively, look for similar projects completed by other people or companies and use them as benchmarks. Then once you come up with your schedule and budget, add an extra buffer.

4. Survivorship bias

Survivorship bias is when we only look at the success stories but fail to take into account all the failures that don't make the headlines. This bias can give us the impression that our chances of success are much higher than they really are. To give you an example, for every start-up that succeeds, hundreds fail.

In other words, trying to discover the key to success by observing successful entrepreneurs might not always be useful. A big part of their success could be the result of luck. After all, if we take a large enough pool of hard-working entrepreneurs, some of them are bound to end up being successful, right?

The point here is not to tell you that *everything* is due to luck, but to help you understand the concept of probabilities so that you are better able to align your thinking with reality. The good news is that luck tends to become less relevant over the long term. This means, if you manage to think fairly well, construct an effective model of reality, and act on it consistently, you're more likely to end up getting "lucky" at some stage.

In *Part III. Empowering your model of reality*, we'll discuss what you can do to "engineer" more luck and further boost your odds of success.

How to deal with survivorship bias

For whatever goal you want to reach, read everything you can about the people who succeed. Try to understand what they did to succeed and what their thought process was during their climb. But don't stop there. Look at the people who failed to achieve that same goal and try to find out why they failed. Then answer the following questions:

- What are all the reasons I could fail?
- What could prevent me from reaching that goal?

Challenges you face could be external obstacles, such as a lack of resources or they could be internal obstacles, such as limiting beliefs or a lack of resourcefulness.

To conclude, learn both from success stories and from failures. This is how you can refine your model of reality and increase the odds of achieving your goals.

5. Dunning-Kruger Effect

Have you noticed that people who know the least sometimes seem to be the most confident? That's the taxi driver who tells you which stocks to pick, the hairdresser who claims to have the solution to complex political issues or the bartender who teaches you how to run your business. This bias has been named the Dunning-Kruger Effect (from the psychologists David Dunning and Justin Kruger who demonstrated this bias through experiments).

As you work toward your goal, one major problem you face is that you don't know what you don't know. This leads you to believe you know more than you actually do which can create serious issues.

As a result, you might become complacent instead of learning more about your goal and refining your assumptions.

How to deal with the Dunning-Kruger Effect

To minimize the consequences of this bias, be willing to question your approach. Continuously learn from feedback and remain humble no matter how experienced you may think you are. Your ability to question everything and your willingness to learn will enable you to refine your model of reality over time. The moment you think you know it all is when your downfall begins—whether you realize this or not.

We'll discuss the importance of being humble and learning from feedback in greater depth in the section, *How your ego affects your thinking*, and in *Part II. Aligning yourself with reality*.

* * *

Action step

Using your action guide, write down how each bias plays out in your life. Aim to give at least one specific example for each bias below:

- Self-serving bias.
- Sunk cost fallacy.
- Planning fallacy.
- Survivorship bias.
- Dunning-Kruger Effect.

C. How your ego affects your thinking

Your ego also plays an important part when it comes to developing accurate thinking. Your ego may lead you to refuse to ask for help, live in denial, avoid failures, or blame other people or circumstances. Such an attitude will severely hamper your ability to perform at your best and achieve your goals.

In this book, we'll define ego as the identity you believe you must protect to maintain your current sense of self. You might think of it as pride.

To improve your thinking, you must let go of your ego. You must be willing to admit when you're wrong. The more you can do so, the more you'll be able to learn and refine your model of reality. Conversely, the more you try to hold onto the idea that you are right, the less you'll learn and the more you risk being out of alignment with reality. Denying reality often leads to mediocrity. By trying to be right, you'll make it much harder to improve.

Now, there are several ways your ego can prevent you from achieving the results you want. An ego out of control might result in you:

1. Living in denial,
2. Refusing to ask for help,
3. Avoiding failures, or
4. Blaming other people or external circumstances.

1. Living in denial

To construct a better model, you must see reality as it is, even when it hurts. You must accept that for things to change, you will have to change. And from your ego's perspective, that's scary.

Unfortunately, being so attached to the way you've always done things might make you unwilling to change your approach. However, failing to look at your issues objectively will prevent you from making the necessary changes in your life.

To give you an example, for months I refused to calculate how much I was making in book royalties. I was too afraid to look at the truth. After quitting my job to write full time, I decided to confront reality. I needed to treat writing as a business, and I started by looking at the numbers. After factoring in editing, proofreading, advertising and all my other costs, I discovered I was actually losing money. Facing that truth enabled me to start making better business decisions and to improve my results over time.

What about you? In what ways are you living in denial? Which areas are you closing your eyes to?

The first step to change anything is to assess the current situation with as much objectivity as possible. Are you willing to do so?

2. Refusing to ask for help

Do you ask for help or do you always try to figure out things on your own?

Many of us are afraid to admit when we need help. We don't want to look bad. We dread letting others know how ignorant or inept we are. However, failing to do so can generate a lot of suffering in our lives. Not to mention that this type of behavior can hinder our progress.

When you fail to ask for help, you risk making decisions that will cost you time and energy. For instance, you may spend hours trying to figure out how to create a blog when you could have asked one of your tech-savvy friends. If you know someone who could give you the information you need or teach you invaluable skills, why not let go of your ego and ask for help?

The point is, it's not only okay to ask for help, it's also often essential. If you don't know something, ask. Most successful people willingly ask for help, so why wouldn't you? By asking more questions, you learn better and faster which enables you to refine your model of reality over time.

Now there are a few reasons you may be afraid of asking which could include:

- Pride,
- The fear of bothering people, or
- The belief you should figure things out for yourself.

Let's briefly go over each of them.

a. Pride

Are you afraid of letting others know how much you are struggling? Do you fear losing face? If that's the case, realize that allowing yourself to be vulnerable will often let you create deeper and more intimate connections with the people around you. Seeking help is not a sign of weakness; it shows that you are willing to grow and open yourself to others. This is what strong people do.

b. Fear of bothering people.

If you're like me, you may not want to bother people with your problems. Perhaps you feel bad because they're busy, or perhaps you think you're not important enough to take up other people's time. If so, this may be a sign that you don't value yourself highly enough. Start noticing these situations and challenge yourself to "bother" others just a little bit more than you currently feel comfortable with.

Also, don't forget that most people are happy to help. We generally love showcasing our expertise. We want to feel useful. So why not "bother" people from time to time? It might feel slightly uncomfortable, but it's a healthy practice that can help you value yourself more.

c. The belief you should figure things out for yourself

Perhaps you believe you should figure things out all by yourself.

This can be a good thing as it stimulates your creativity and develops your resourcefulness—a key element to achieving a higher level of success. However, there are also times when you are far better off asking for support. You can't afford the luxury of reinventing the wheel every time you attempt something new. If the people around you have skills and knowledge you can benefit from, why not ask for their guidance?

Before I attended business school back in 2013, I didn't know anything about business and could barely use a spreadsheet. Too ashamed to reveal my poor skills, I would let others create spreadsheets during group work, or I would find ways to get them to share their files with me. This behavior not only prevented me from honing my skills, but also made me feel inadequate. This is a pattern I've seen play out many times in my life. It works as follow:

- I assume I should know how to do something (even though I have no experience doing it),
- I feel ashamed of myself for not knowing how to do it,
- I try hard to hide my "inadequacy" while feeling terrible about myself,
- Not asking for help, I struggle to improve,
- The skill gap between me and others further widens, and
- I end up feeling even worse about myself.

I believe this is a pattern that many people with low self-esteem go through. So, if the above process sounds familiar, notice it. And remember, it doesn't have to be that way.

Most successful people reach out for help. They recognize it as the best way to attain better results faster. They also understand that mutual help is a wonderful way to create deeper and more meaningful relationships with their spouses, kids, friends or colleagues. It makes them feel part of a community.

In short, by not asking for help, you risk feeling isolated and powerless. Almost inevitably, some people out there have the answer to your question. Why not find them and ask for their support? This might be the smartest and most mature thing you can do.

3. Avoiding failure

Are you afraid of failure? Are you scared of looking bad?

Failing means you're trying something new, and your ego usually doesn't like that. It prefers maintaining the status quo. However, to achieve any meaningful goal, you'll have to grow. If you were already the person you needed to be to reach your goals, you would already have achieved them, wouldn't you?

But you haven't.

Change is the only constant in this world. Everything either grows or decays. If you don't maintain your house, it will eventually fall apart. If you don't grow your business, you'll lose market share to your competitors and if you don't make an effort to improve, you'll tend to become worse. Therefore, to grow and move toward your ideal life, you need to challenge yourself by experimenting with new things. This entails a willingness to fail.

There is no such thing as failure

Many people try to avoid failing at all costs, but this is not how to design your ideal life. The most successful people on this planet understand the value of failure. They are willing to "fail" as many times as necessary until they achieve their goals.

In truth, failure is something to use, not to avoid. Failure is the feedback mechanism you need to refine your model of reality. You *need* failures so that you can adjust your trajectory and hit your goals. The same way that pain tells you something is wrong with your body, "failures" tell you something might be off with your approach. As you learn to see failures as feedback from reality, you'll find it easier to persevere until you reach your final destination.

Note that failure isn't personal. You don't "fail", you tried something that didn't work. If it didn't work, try something else. Ask for feedback. Consult experts. Find a mentor. Tweak your plan. Or try just one more time.

The bottom line is, stop being afraid of failure. Use every single one of your so-called failures to refine your model of reality. And keep adjusting your trajectory until you travel from where you are now to where you want to be in the future.

4. Blaming other people and circumstances

Another tendency you might have is to play the victim. The problem is, when you act like a victim, you rob yourself of an opportunity to take more responsibility for your life and make positive changes. Being a victim means you abandon your power and give it away to other people or circumstances.

A good way to explain victimhood is to imagine a spectrum with "personal responsibility" on the far left side and "blame" on the far right side. The more you take personal responsibility, the less you blame other people or external circumstances and vice-versa. These concepts are mutually exclusive.

So why do you like to play the victim? Being a victim probably:

- Enables you to maintain the illusion you're right (your ego hates being wrong), and
- Allows you to do nothing about your situation. Accepting the idea that you may be partly responsible would force you to do something which may require a lot of time and energy.

Now I'm not saying other people or circumstances are never

obstacles standing between you and your goals. What I *am* saying is that the more you seek responsibility for everything that happens to you, the more you empower yourself and the better chance you have to improve your situation.

For instance, blaming your lack of success on a difficult childhood will not help you design your ideal future. On the other hand, by being willing to ask yourself what you can do about your current situation, you'll come up with a variety of actions you can start taking today.

Part of thinking accurately entails acknowledging the idea that you have the power to change your life. And this starts by focusing on what you can do rather than looking for who or what is to blame. This is how you can achieve tangible results in the real world.

* * *

Action step

Using your action guide, write down one specific example from your personal life for each ego activity below:

- Living in denial.
- Refusing to ask for help.
- Avoiding failures, and
- Blaming other people or external circumstances.

Then write down what you could do to deal with each of these four ego traps.

D. How your emotions distort your thinking

Inaccurate thinking can also be the result of a disempowering emotional state. Our emotions can distort both our thinking and the way we behave. For instance, when you feel good about yourself, you are more creative and have more energy to take the actions needed to achieve your goals. Conversely, when you're feeling like a failure, you have no motivation and invite in more and more negative thinking. In this negative condition, everything seems gloomy and you're unable to think clearly or make sound decisions.

In short, when you're under the spell of negative emotions, you tend to lose your sense of perspective. Therefore, if you want to develop accurate thinking, you need to learn how to manage your emotions more effectively.

1. Key characteristics of negative emotions

Below are some characteristics of negative emotions you need to be aware of:

a. Negative emotions act as a spell

When you're under the influence of negative emotions, it might seem impossible to break free from them. You may feel the urge to focus on the same disempowering thoughts repeatedly.

b. Negative emotions filter your experiences

Negative emotions act as a filter that taints the quality of your experiences. During a negative episode, you perceive every experience through this filter. Although the world outside may remain the same, you will experience it in a completely different way based on how you feel.

For instance, when you're sad, you might not enjoy the food you eat, the movie you see, or the activities in which you engage. You only see the negative side of things and end up feeling trapped and powerless. On the other hand, when you're in a positive mood, everything in life appears better. Food tastes great, you're naturally friendlier, and you enjoy all the activities you partake in.

c. Negative emotions attract more negative emotions

When you're in a negative emotional state, you will begin to attract more emotions on a similar "wave" (i.e., more negative emotions). For instance, you might be in a bad mood because your boss yelled at you at work. This may lead you to think about some issues you have with your partner. You may then remember your back pain and start obsessing over it. As a result, you will feel even worse.

2. Four tips to help you overcome emotional traps

By now, you understand that your emotions can distort your thinking. If you don't keep them under control, they will wreak havoc in your life. To manage your emotions more effectively, I encourage you to do the following:

Tip #1—Recognize the idea that you are not your emotions. Your emotions can never define you. For instance, being sad for months doesn't make you a lesser person than you were when you were happy. Emotions are like clouds hiding the sun. The sun is *always* there. You are the sun. Sure, your emotions can trick you beyond anything you can imagine—and they will—but they *cannot* change your essence.

Tip #2—Refrain from clustering negative emotions together. Negative emotions attract more negative emotions. Thus, start noticing whenever you start clustering issues together (e.g., having back pain, hating your job and being in the middle of an argument with your partner). Then look at each issue separately. By doing so, you will realize that, when taken independently, these issues might not be as big an issue as you thought, or they are at least more manageable. Don't stack negative thoughts together. Instead, compartmentalize them and deal with them individually.

Tip #3—Avoid making important decisions when under the spell of strong emotions. Your emotions distort your thinking. This goes for both negative *and* positive emotions. Consequently, avoid making any major decisions when you're experiencing highs (feeling ecstatic) or lows (feeling depressed, hopeless, angry, et cetera). Instead, wait until you revert to a more neutral emotional state. You'll think much more clearly and will make better decisions as a result. For example:

- Don't decide to give up on your dreams when you feel depressed. Wait until you feel better before making such important decisions.
- Don't reply to an email that makes you angry. Instead, wait at least 24 hours.
- Don't make any promises or major decisions just after receiving great news, (e.g., winning the lottery).

If you avoid making any serious decisions when under the spell of emotions, it will save you a lot of trouble.

Tip #4—Cultivate self-compassion. How often do you make yourself miserable by figuratively beating yourself up? The worst time to do so is when you already feel bad. This is why I like to adopt what I call the "I'll beat myself up later policy". In other words, I give myself permission to be hard on myself later, but *not* when I'm in a negative emotional state. Instead, I show myself some much needed compassion. That's what I encourage you to do as well.

We'll discuss how to cultivate self-compassion in greater depth in *Part III. Empowering your model of reality.*

Use the tips above to help you manage your emotions better, and you'll be able to make better life decisions.

* * *

Action step

Complete the exercises in your action guide:

- Remember a time when everything felt hopeless or gloomy, and you didn't believe you could be happy again. Then realize your negative emotions eventually faded away.
- Think of three current challenges in your life one after the other. How does each make you feel? Now, visualize three things you're grateful for or excited about. Feel better?
- Think of one poor decision you made as a result of negative emotions (anger, hopelessness, frustration et cetera) or positive emotions (joy, euphoria, excitement, et cetera).
- For one full minute give yourself some words of encouragement. Remind yourself that you're doing well, that you have noble intentions and that you're proud of all the things you've accomplished. How does it make you feel?

Now, let's explore additional ways you distort your thinking by reviewing common negative thought patterns.

3. Three common negative thought patterns to avoid

As human beings, we all fall prey to a certain number of negative thought patterns. Understanding these patterns will help you manage your emotions further and ensure you think more clearly.

Thought pattern #1—Generalization. This is when you oversimplify things instead of having a more nuanced approach. You can often tell when you generalize by noticing your use of such words as "always" or "never". Some examples are:

Always:

- I'm always late.
- I'm always wrong.
- I'm always the one who ....
- Why does it always happen to me?

Never:

- I will never be happy again.
- I never get things right.
- I will never be able to find a job like this one.

Have you ever made any of the above statements?

This type of generalization is not only inaccurate, it also leads you to feel bad about yourself. You're not always late, are you? You may be late more often than you'd like to be, but you're also on time on many occasions. Yes, bad things may happen to you occasionally, but this is not the default position. Many other people face similar issues, and some probably more than you.

Take note of whenever you use words such as "always" or "never" because they often indicate you're distorting the truth. You may do this to elicit sympathy or to avoid taking responsibility for your current situation. In any case, generalizing behavior such as this distorts your thinking and hampers you from achieving your future goals.

* * *

Action step

Whenever you find yourself generalizing, reframe the sentence to reflect reality more accurately. See the examples below:

I'm always late. —> I may be late more often than I'd like to be, but I'm also on time on many occasions.

I'm always the one people make fun of. —> People might make fun of me occasionally, but I'm certainly not the only one, and it doesn't happen all the time.

I never get things right. —> I get things wrong on some occasions, but I get things right many times, too.

Thought pattern #2—All or nothing thinking. This is another toxic pattern you may be falling for. All or nothing thinking is when you believe you need to get something or you'll be unhappy, unworthy of love, et cetera. All or nothing thinking is when you believe your own happiness depends on a specific event external to you. Some examples are:

- I will only be happy when I get that job.
- If I can't achieve that goal, my life is not worth living.
- I need to marry that person or I will never be happy.

This is a distortion of the way life works. To live a successful and happy life, there isn't one specific thing you need to do, to be, or to have. You're not just given one shot in life. In truth:

- Your lifelong dream that fails to materialize might actually open doors to new opportunities you didn't even know existed.
- That dream job you didn't get may lead you to a new exciting career you didn't even think possible.
- Being rejected by the person you thought was your one

true love may lead you to meet someone even more amazing.

Life isn't an all or nothing event. This is an inaccurate way of thinking. When you find yourself making your happiness or self-worth dependent on one event, thing or person, take note. Remember there are *always* opportunities out there. And to be happy, there is no specific thing you need to do or to have. If one thing doesn't work, something else will. So never lose your enthusiasm and avoid beating yourself up when things don't work out. Instead, keep believing in yourself, keep appreciating all the things you already have, and keep doing your best.

* * *

Action step

Using your action guide, look at each area of your life and see how you may succumb to the all or nothing thinking.

Thought pattern #3—Dramatization. Dramatization is when you imagine things are far worse than they actually are. We all exaggerate things from time to time, don't we? We make a big deal of things that aren't. This is especially true when we are tired, ill or a little down. However, dramatization is inaccurate thinking.

Imagine that your boss just yelled at you. You now picture yourself being fired. Before realizing it, you've created a mental movie of yourself being homeless. You see your wife abandoning you and, you become scared. This is a little bit of an exaggeration, isn't it? It seems as though you've skipped a whole lot of steps that would need to happen for you to find yourself in that situation.

This type of thinking probably happens because of the way our brain works. Our brain is designed to give a lot of weight to potential threats which is how we were able to survive as a species.

To survive and reproduce, our ancestors needed to identify any and every threat. When in doubt, they would assume the worst. It made more sense for them to mistake a piece of wood for a snake than the opposite.

Unfortunately, our brains still work the same way today. So be aware of your natural tendency to envision the worse, thank your ancestors—you wouldn't be here if it weren't for their survival skills—, and think more rationally and positively. Most of the things you worry about will never happen.

To learn how to manage your emotions more effectively and in more detail, refer to my book, *Master Your Emotions*.

* * *

Action step

Remember one time you worried about something that never happened. Write it down in your action guide.

In summary, to develop accurate thinking you must become aware of all the ways your thought process might be flawed. When you distort reality through poor and inaccurate thinking, the result is almost always mental suffering and poor performance.

Now, let's see the specific things you can do to align with reality more effectively and achieve tangible results.

PART II

ALIGNING YOURSELF WITH REALITY

Do you wish the world could be different with no wars or misery? I certainly do.

Unfortunately, the reality is that wars are occurring right now. And hundreds of millions of people live in misery. Now what if I tell you things are exactly the way they are, even though it's not the way you want them to be? But I hear you ask, "Thibaut, how can you be okay with the way the world is?"

People suffer and that is really unfortunate, but it also happens to be the truth.

Reality simply *is*. And refusing to accept that as a fact is not only a sign of insanity, but also a sign of arrogance. It's like saying the world should be the way we picture it just because that's what *we* want.

Truth being said, reality can never be wrong. It has never been and never will be. How could what actually exists not exist?

Now, please bear with me. Understanding the concept that reality can't be wrong is critical because when we fail to acknowledge reality for what it is, we live in denial. And usually nothing constructive comes from living in denial.

1

ACCEPTING REALITY AS IT IS

The first step to achieving better results in any area of your life is to accept reality as it is. Put differently, we need to cultivate the most accurate model of reality possible. Because if your model is flawed, you'll take ineffective or even counter-productive action and will achieve mediocre results at best. In short, the best way to play the whole game of life is to align yourself with reality. To "win" the game you need to know the rules—or at least have a solid understanding of what they are. This starts by accepting reality as it is, not by thinking it should be any different.

1) Should vs. is

There should be no poverty. All people should be treated equally. I should make more money. Have you ever thought along these lines?

The problem with believing things *should* be different is that it can put you in a disempowering state. It can also lead you to overlook reality and only live in an imaginary ideal world where everybody is happy and successful.

Now I'm not saying there is anything wrong with envisioning a better world. I'm all for it. However, before you do that, it is important you take a sincere and objective look at the reality in front of you. Ignoring reality will not help you take the appropriate action.

2) Should vs. could

A better way of thinking is to replace "should" with "could". While "should" implies that things aren't the way they're supposed to be, "could" offers possibilities, not judgment. You can choose to explore these possibilities, or you can reject them.

For instance, if you say, "I should be working", it implies that something is wrong with the current reality of you not working. You're emitting a judgment (i.e., you're lazy or undisciplined because you're not working). On the other hand, if you say, "I could be working", you accept the reality that you're not currently working. Then you're inviting yourself to work if you choose to. Can you see the difference between the two statements?

The point is, you can "should" yourself as much as you want, but it won't help. It will only lead you to feel guilty. Therefore, start noticing whenever you use the word "should". Then try using "could" instead and see how it makes you feel. Below are examples of the way our thinking can change based on whether we use "should" or "could".

- I *should* be married. —> Something is wrong with me for not being married.
- I *could* be married. —> At my age, many people are married, but I'm not. I may choose to get married at some stage in the future. But I may also choose not to get married at all if that's not something I want.

- I *should* be making more money. —> Something is wrong

44

with me for not being able to make more money. The world is unfair to me.

- I *could* be making more money. —> I'm not making as much money as I want right now, but there are things I can do, starting today, that will help me generate more money in the future, such as asking for a raise, changing career or creating my own business.

- There *should* be no war. —> Something is wrong with the world. It's a violent place. It should be peaceful.
- There *could* be no war. —> If we work toward developing a more peaceful society, perhaps in the future, wars might disappear or occur less frequently.

The bottom line is, in order to develop an accurate model of reality, you must accept that things are exactly the way they're supposed to be right now, whether you like it or not.

This is the first step: accepting reality as it is.

Then once you recognize things are the way they *are*, you can start envisioning a better future and create a blueprint to improve things you wish would be different.

* * *

Action step

Complete the following exercises using your action guide:

- Write down at least three "should" statements you often use.
- Replace "should" with "could".
- See how it makes you feel and how it changes your thought process.

2

UNCOVERING YOUR ASSUMPTIONS

A. Identifying your assumptions

In Part I, we discussed how your inaccurate assumptions can lead you to think inaccurately and develop a flawed model of reality. Now let's see how to identify your assumptions in greater depth so you can develop specific and achievable goals.

Whenever you set a life goal, you immediately start making assumptions regarding what you need to do to achieve it. Your assumptions may be that this goal is unrealistic and that you will never reach it. Or they may suggest that to obtain a specific outcome, you will need to do X, Y or Z.

For instance, let's assume you've written a book and want it to become a best-seller. Your first idea might be to go on national TV. You think you will sell thousands of copies that way. Or perhaps you believe that because you spent so much time and energy writing your book—and care so much about your readers—, it will sell gazillions of copies. It's just a matter of time before people find out about your books, right?

In short, for any of your goals, you will make initial assumptions regarding the best strategy to reach it, but these assumptions will often be inaccurate. Now what do you think will happen if you decide to take action based on these weak assumptions? You'll waste your time and energy and will probably fail to attain your goal. Sadly, this is what many people do, often unknowingly.

Let's return to our previous example of writing a best-selling book. One of my writer friends went on a national TV to promote his book. He was excited and thought it would lead to a massive spike in sales. Unfortunately, it had a negligible impact on sales. It turned out that appearing on national TV wasn't the magic solution, at least not in this specific case. Another writer friend spent years writing his first book, expecting to sell loads of copies due to the sheer quality of his work. That didn't happen either.

The bottom line is, before you start working on any goal, you need to identify all your erroneous assumptions. Then you need to replace them with more accurate ones. The better you become at this "game", the more likely you are to hit your target.

* * *

Action step

Using your action guide, select one important goal and make a list of all the assumptions you may be making about it. Please note we'll keep using this goal for future exercises.

To help you identify your assumptions, please refer to the questions below:

- What are your assumptions regarding the best ways to reach this goal?
- What strategies do you assume will work and why?
- Do you think it will be easy or hard, and why?

- How long do you think it will take you to reach this goal and why?

B. Testing your assumptions

Once you have identified the assumptions you're making regarding your goal, the next step is to assess each one to see how accurate it is. Don't worry if you're unsure about the accuracy of your assumptions. That's normal. As you do more research and gather invaluable information, you'll be able to improve the quality and accuracy of your assumptions. We'll work on this throughout the book, but for now, it's time to work through the assessment process. And remember, there are no wrong answers.

Action step

- Look at the list of assumptions you just wrote down in your action guide.
- Next to each assumption, write down the accuracy score you would give it on a scale from 1 to 10, (one being completely inaccurate and 10 being one hundred percent accurate).

3

REFINING YOUR MODEL OF REALITY

By now, you should have identified your current assumptions. You should also have given each of them an accuracy score. The next step is to challenge these assumptions and work on implementing more accurate ones. Below are the steps you can follow to refine your model of reality:

- Revising your assumptions.
- Sharpening your thinking by asking yourself questions.
- Interviewing experienced people.
- Doing your own research.
- Being curious.
- Listening to your emotions.

A. Revising your assumptions

Forget about your previous assumptions for a moment and let's start over. To do so, ask yourself the following questions, "What do I really know for sure?" and "What is really true?"

Let's say you enjoy writing and would love to do it full time.

However, your original assumption is that you can't make money from writing. You'll need a regular job or a few side hustles to pay the bills. But is this assumption true? And how do you know this for sure? Let's do some research and find it out, shall we?

As you do your research, you'll discover that most writers don't make much money. In fact, most self-published authors sell fewer than 250 copies of their books. For traditionally published authors, it might be a few thousand copies.

However, your research will also tell you that thousands of writers *do* earn a living solely from their books. In fact, some are making six or seven-figure incomes. While these writers represent a small minority of the author population, they do show you it's possible.

Okay. So, you now know that thousands of writers are making a living from their writing. But is that a lot? Considering the number of aspiring writers, it isn't. Does it mean you should give up? Not necessarily. It means you need to be realistic and work smart.

To further refine your model, keep digging deeper by asking yourself, "What do I know for sure about these full-time writers?" As you study them, you'll find out commonalities that may come in handy if you choose to become a full-time writer yourself.

What's more, the same process works for any other goal.

The point I'm making is that the more you drill down, the more quality information you'll find and the more likely you'll be to take the appropriate actions to reach your goal. Remember, the idea behind refining your model of reality is to reduce the amount of luck required to achieve your desired results.

In conclusion, the first step toward improving your model of reality is to ask yourself what you know for sure. After that, you need to do the necessary research to find the accurate answers that will help you attain your goal.

* * *

Action step

In your action guide, write down your answers to the questions below:

- What do you know for sure regarding your goal?
- How can you be so certain?

B. Sharpening your thinking by asking yourself questions

Another way to improve your model of reality is by asking yourself smart questions to guide your thinking and improve your results. Ultimately, the most important question you want to find answers to is:

How do I know whether my goal is realistic and whether I will achieve it or not?

Answering the list of questions below will help you do that. Look at your previous goal or select one of your major goals and make sure you answer each of them using your action guide.

Here is the list:

1) Do I believe I will achieve my goal?

On a scale from 1 to 10 (one being not at all confident and ten being absolutely certain), how confident are you that you will reach your goal? The more confident you are, the better. A high level of certainty will lead you to take greater action and will help you keep going despite multiple setbacks.

If your answer is below 7, what could you do to boost your confidence? Could you adjust the scope of your goal, change it a little, or give yourself more time? If your answer is 7 or 8, that's an encouraging start. Now how could you make it 9 or 10?

In *Part III. Empowering Your Model of Reality*, we'll discuss in greater detail how you can develop rock-solid confidence to help you improve your confidence score.

2) Do I have a track record of achieving similar goals?

If you've already achieved major goals in the past, you'll build confidence in your ability to reach your current goal. If not, don't worry. As you keep setting and achieving small goals consistently, your confidence will grow. Over time, you'll achieve bigger and bigger goals. For more on this subject, refer to the section, *Achieving goals consistently.*

3) What makes me think I will reach this goal? What concrete evidence or tangible results are there to support this claim?

The simple fact you're pursuing your goals means you believe there is a chance you'll reach them, but what makes you think so? Where is the evidence?

To give you a personal example, one of the reasons I decided to write full time is that I received great reviews and encouraging messages for my first book, *Goal Setting*. Below is one of them:

"I recently read your book on goal setting. Tremendous! Keep it up man, you have a great gift of synthesizing information into pure crystal clarity."

If the majority of people had told me my book sucked, I might not have gone on to become a full-time writer.

If you've been pursuing a goal for years, but have yet to receive positive feedback from strangers as well as family and friends, it's unlikely you'll reach your goal unless you change your approach.

If you're offering a product or service, positive feedback isn't enough. You want to get customers to:

1. Spend their hard-earned money on your product/service, *and*
2. Give you positive feedback.

If you can do both, it's a sign you might be on to something.

So, where is your evidence?

4) Do the people around me believe I will achieve my goal?

The longer you stay committed and the greater number of important milestones you reach, the more likely it will be for the people around you to take you seriously. If you find these people to be unsupportive, it may be a sign that you must boost your confidence to make them believe your story. An effective way to do so is to take more action.

If despite early successes, your friends or family members are still unsupportive, perhaps you need to start surrounding yourself with more positive people. We'll discuss how to do this in greater detail in *Part III. Empowering your model of Reality.*

5) Do I have the energy and/or time required to achieve this goal within the set timeframe?

For you to achieve any meaningful endeavor, you will need to devote a considerable amount of time and energy to it. Can you really dedicate enough time and energy to your goal right now? If not, consider revising its scope and/or setting more realistic deadlines. Remember, we're terrible at assessing the amount of time or energy needed to attain our goals.

6) How many people have achieved this goal before? How many people are trying to achieve it now?

You want to know how tough the competition is. The more slots are available, the easier it will be to achieve success. For instance, only a small number of people can become professional singers, but tens of thousands of people can be teachers or engineers. If you enter a field with limited openings, be prepared to do the work.

7) Who has achieved this goal before?

Do you know people who have achieved your goal or a similar one? If not, can you find the best books, courses or seminars from people who have been there and done that?

Remember, the last thing you want to do is reinvent the wheel. You have more important things to do with your time.

8) Why is this goal important to me?

Why are you pursuing this specific goal as opposed to another one? Emotions are more important than logic. The greater the number of emotional reasons you have behind your goal, the more motivated you'll be.

For instance, there were many reasons I was determined to build a successful online business around personal development. The benefits that appealed to me the most were:

- Being able to make money doing what I love,
- Feeling as though I'm making a positive impact,
- Having the freedom to travel around the world,
- Being able to take vacations whenever I want, and
- Having the opportunities to scale my income.

When I combined all these reasons, I felt highly motivated. What about you? Why is your goal so important to you? The more reasons you have to reach your goal, the better.

9) If I keep doing what I'm doing every day will I achieve my goals? If not, what exactly needs to change?

This is a great question and one I like to ask myself on a regular basis. When you ask yourself this question, be completely honest with yourself. If you struggle to find an answer, keep refining your model of reality by asking smart questions, finding role models, gathering case studies and so on.

10) What are the best approaches/strategies to follow?

Whatever goal you're trying to achieve, there are often a large number of tactics you could experiment with. For instance, let's say you want to find clients to coach. You could:

- Attend networking events,
- Organize free seminars,
- Offer free sessions to promote your coaching program,
- Build your presence on LinkedIn by posting valuable content in your niche,
- Write a book in your area of expertise to get qualified leads,
- Be a guest on various podcasts in your industry,
- Create a YouTube Channel to gather leads,
- Create a sales page and drive traffic to it by using ads, or
- Create a website and do SEO optimization to receive traffic from search engines.

Now if you try to do all these things at once, you will likely fail. The best approach for you will depend on things such as:

- What you think will be most effective based on your own research,
- What you enjoy doing the most, and
- What you're good at.

For instance, if you're an extrovert, you might enjoy creating YouTube videos, attending networking events or organizing seminars. On the other hand, if you're an introvert, you might prefer running ads or writing online content.

11) What does my intuition tell me to do?

If you quiet your mind for a moment and listen to your intuition, you might find answers to your questions. For instance, you might experience a nagging feeling telling you that a specific approach isn't right for you. Conversely, you might feel as though you're doing exactly what you're supposed to do. Practice listening to your inner voice. Intuition is often your values, ethics and strengths talking to you and suggesting the right path for you to follow.

Answering the questions above will enable you to come up with a more effective approach for your goals.

* * *

Action step

Answer all the questions above and add the answers to your action guide.

C. Interviewing experienced people

The third step is to gather information from knowledgeable people. The key is to ask them smart questions that will enable you to improve your model.

Below are some examples of questions to ask.

1) How does this work?

For instance, how do things work in your industry? This question will help you grasp the big picture. Having a decent understanding of how things work will help you make better decisions and prevent you from getting lost in the details. You want to look at the whole forest, not just at one specific tree.

2) *What are the biggest assumptions you make? And how do you know these are accurate or effective?*

By asking the experts how they know their assumptions are correct, they will have to explain their thought process, giving you a deeper insight into their model of reality. Note that it probably took them years to refine their model, both through theoretical knowledge and actual experience. As such, it is bound to be much more accurate than yours.

Bonus tip: Now just because they have a lot of experience doesn't mean their model of reality is actually one hundred percent accurate. Some of their assumptions may be erroneous. As such, it's a good idea to interview many people to get as wide an overview as possible.

3) *What do I need to understand that I may not understand yet?*

This question will give the interviewee the opportunity to mention anything he or she may have forgotten. Furthermore, it will ensure you're not missing any important points and help you avoid making rookie mistakes.

4) *If you were in my shoes what would you do?*

This question will allow you to receive more practical advice. By being invited to think from a different perspective, the interviewee may provide you with more valuable information.

5) *How did you get where you are?*

This question will help you zero in on what the interviewee identifies as key to their success. But once again, it doesn't mean this person is completely right in his or her assessment. To take things one step further, you can ask them why they think each factor is important and how they know this is the case.

6) If you were to start all over again, what would you do differently to generate success more quickly?

This question will encourage your interviewees to identify the key factors leading to their success in greater detail. To pinpoint the few key activities that delivered and continue delivering tangible results, they will have to think more deeply.

7) If you had to choose only one activity to focus on, which one would give you the best results?

People tend to take on too many things instead of focusing on a few key activities. This question will help your interviewee further identify what really matters, providing you with additional information in the process.

If you can't interview people, watch interviews online, read autobiographies, et cetera, and search for the answers to the questions mentioned above. This leads us to our next point.

* * *

Action step

Complete at least one of the following exercises (and preferably both).

- Ask each question to the relevant person/people and write down the answers in your action guide.
- Watch interviews and/or read biographies and try answering the above questions based on the information you've gathered.

D. Doing your own research

The fourth step is to conduct extensive research which involves looking for case studies and finding the highest quality information possible. To do so, start by asking yourself what is the highest quality of information out there?

Perhaps it's one or two books written by the best experts in that field. Perhaps it's research papers from prestigious universities. Or perhaps it's a course created by the number one authority in your field. The key is to be strategic in the way you look for information. If you fail to do so, you risk:

- Feeling overwhelmed and drowning under the sea of information available, and
- Consuming low-quality information that could mislead you or prevent you from achieving tangibly positive results.

By taking a moment to identify the right approach, you'll save yourself time and energy down the road. For example, as I was pursuing my goals of becoming a full-time writer, I read books from some of the most successful indie authors. One piece of advice I kept hearing them say was: the best marketing tool is to write another book. Many successful indie authors produce books consistently. They often choose to write another book over revising an older one. So I decided to do the same.

Now it doesn't mean everybody should do the same thing. Some writers might choose to spend most of their time marketing an existing book to land speaking gigs or sell their products or services. This may be an effective strategy, too.

Earlier, we discovered that while most writers don't make much money, a few thousand make a decent living from their writing. As we delve deeper with our research, we'll come across a Facebook group called 20BooksTo50k®. This group contains over 35,000 writers, some of whom are full-time authors. Being a member of this group, reading the all-star threads and taking consistent action, gives us a lead over the crowd.

Detailed research is critical. It will give you an edge over your competitors. No matter how competitive your field may be, only a fraction of the "contestants" will make the effort to find the right information. Among these people, a tiny minority will act on the information they find and have a strong enough mindset to succeed. It's not to say you are absolutely guaranteed to achieve your goal, but it does mean there are many things you *can* do to improve your odds of success. And doing your own detailed research is a great start.

So when it comes to achieving your wildest goals, leave nothing out. Do everything in your power to gather the right information and cultivate the most accurate model of reality possible.

In Part III of this book, *Empowering your model of reality*, we'll discuss the specific things you can do to turbocharge your model and maximize your chances of success.

To learn more on that topic, you can also refer to my book, *Success is Inevitable.*

Now let's see how you can find the right information to refine your model of reality.

1. How to find high-quality information

As the saying goes, "garbage in, garbage out". To ensure you build the most accurate model of reality possible, you need quality input. That is, you must gather the highest quality information available.

To do so, I invite you to bear in mind the hierarchy of information I introduced in *Master Your Focus*, the third book in the "Master

Your ..." series. Roughly speaking, information can be sorted as follows (from low quality to high quality):

- **Blogs/articles/YouTube videos** - provide tips but often remain superficial or lack structure, making it difficult to achieve long-term results with the information presented.
- **Free courses** - offer a little information and in a more structured way.
- **Books** - can offer in-depth information, but they are only effective when the reader completes the recommended exercises.
- **Paid courses** - offer in-depth information in a well-structured way, increasing the odds the students will take action. Also, because people pay for them, they have "buy-in" and tend to take more action.
- **High-end courses** - can offer in-depth, high-quality information in a highly structured way. These courses can also provide group coaching sessions and other activities that strengthen accountability and generate excitement. They encourage people to take serious action due to the higher entry price.
- **Mentoring** - allows students to absorb years of knowledge through face-to-face interaction with a highly experienced tutor. Potential benefits include intense shortening of the learning curve, implementation of a highly effective strategy and a powerful shift in the student's mindset.
- **Mastermind groups** - allow students to learn from highly successful people with similar goals and extensive knowledge. They foster accountability and boost motivation.
- **One-on-one coaching** - allows students to work individually with an expert and received instant feedback as well as highly customized advice. These sessions offer

access to the best strategy available and create strong accountability.

For major goals, you might consider purchasing courses or working with a coach or mentor. Whatever you choose to do, seek ways to shorten your learning curve.

* * *

Action step

Using your action guide, answer the following question:

What is the highest quality of information out there and where can you find it?

Now let's see how to ensure that the information you gather is not only high-quality, but also relevant to your situation.

2. How to find the right information for *you*

Finding high-quality information isn't enough. What's even more important is making sure this information is what *you* really need right now and that it will work for *you*. To do so:

- Make sure you have a clearly defined goal,
- Understand how the information applies to you specifically, and
- Ensure the information is up to date.

a. Make sure you have a clearly defined goal

The first thing to do before you can gather relevant information is to know what you want it to do for you. Why do you need it in the first place?

Do you want to learn about the theory, or do you need practical steps to follow right away? Do you want in-depth knowledge on a topic you're already knowledgeable in, or do you want easily digestible information to get you started?

The information you need will vary based on your goals and your initial expertise. Therefore, knowing what you're trying to achieve will not only help you find the right information, but it will also ensure it's the right information for *you* right now.

* * *

Action step

Using your action guide, answer the following questions:

- What exactly is my goal? What do I hope to create by using this information? For instance, it could be writing a research paper, starting a new diet or teaching a concept to someone.
- If I could obtain the perfect information that would guarantee I achieve my goal, what would it look like? How would it be structured? These questions will help you identify the information you really need and come up with the best strategy to find that information (e.g., asking a friend, consulting specific documents, visiting relevant websites, et cetera).

b. Understand how the information applies to *you*

One of the issues with any piece of information is that the source, whether a person or an organization, is inevitably biased. The creator of any piece of content has their own life experiences, values, personality and agenda. As such, their recommendations might not be what you need right now. After all, you also have your own experiences, values, personality and goals.

Therefore because someone pitches a seemingly once-in-a-lifetime opportunity during a webinar, it doesn't mean you should jump in, no matter how excited you feel in the moment. Instead, you should take time to select goals that align with your values, passion, personal mission and/or natural strengths. Otherwise, the opportunities you go after are unlikely to work for you.

Below are a couple of questions to help you select the information that can apply to you specifically.

Does the recommended blueprint or advice apply in my specific case?

In other words, do you have the experience, strengths or personality needed to make this method work for you? While a strategy might be effective for others, it might not be effective for *you*—at least not right now.

Perhaps the methodology plays on your weakness rather than leverages your strengths. For instance, you may be naturally gifted at writing, but terrible at speaking. If so, being told you should cold-call prospects to grow your business might not work for you. Or perhaps you lack the experience required to make a particular strategy work. If so, you may need more foundation level information before you can move on to more advanced strategies.

Do I have a genuine desire to take action on what I've learned?

If for whatever reason, you don't feel motivated, determine whether the approach you're taking is the right one for you. Perhaps it's something you think you *should* do rather than something you *want* to do. Or perhaps you find the approach unethical which creates inner resistance and prevents you from moving forward. Also, whenever necessary, revise your strategy or change your goal. Forcing yourself to push forward with a goal that is uninspiring or out of alignment with your core values will, in most cases, lead you to give up sooner or later.

* * *

Action step

Answer the question below using your action guide:

- Does the recommended blueprint, program or advice apply in my specific case?
- Do I have the desire to take action on that information? If not, why not? What changes do I need to make?

c. Ensure the information is up to date

A piece of content might be outdated by the time you read it, and realizing this isn't always straightforward. For example, in my industry, people who sold loads of books five years ago may offer outdated courses. These courses can leave many aspiring writers confused. Sure, they may contain useful information, but the obsolete part of the course can also prevent the aspiring writer from developing an accurate model of reality—*as it is today.*

The point is, you should make sure the information you're consuming is still relevant and valid. Otherwise, it may leave you overwhelmed and confused. In many cases, technology-related information can become outdated pretty quickly. For instance, online marketing strategies that worked six months ago may not work that well today.

Whenever you consume information, look at the date it was created. Then ask yourself whether it is still relevant. Remember, inaccurate information will lead you to take ineffective action which will prevent you achieving your goals. To enhance the accuracy of your model of reality, make a conscious effort to gather the latest information that is relevant to *you*.

Action step

To ensure the information is up to date, you can ask yourself some of the questions below using your action guide:

- Is this information still relevant today?
- How can I make sure it actually is still relevant?
- If I'm unable to answer the two questions above, do I know someone who has the answer?

Bonus tip: how to deal with being overwhelmed

With the volume of information readily available today, it is easy to feel lost. Feeling overwhelmed is often a sign you should pause and think. It could be an invitation to reevaluate your overall strategy, reconnect with your original vision or reorganize your notetaking or filing system. Therefore whenever you feel overwhelmed, take note. It's usually an indication that you're consuming more information than you can swallow right now. If so, follow the steps below:

- Stop what you're doing,
- Take a step back and refocus on the big picture,
- Identify what you're trying to accomplish and what the final output should look like, and
- Pinpoint the specific information you need to reach your goal.

I encourage you to take a pen and piece of paper to answer the questions above.

E. Being curious

To refine your model of reality, you must be on constant lookout for new information that could help you reach your goals. Now, this doesn't mean you should fall for the Shiny Object Syndrome and jump from one potentially exciting development to the next. However, it does mean that you should observe trends and keep a close eye on what successful people are doing in your area of interest. To achieve demanding goals, you must be willing to become the most knowledgeable person in your field. Therefore:

- If you want to make money with your art, learn everything you can about the way to do so.
- If you want to be a coach, learn everything you can about that profession.
- If you want to be a trader, learn everything you can about trading.

While this is common sense, it's not always common practice. To build a proper model of reality that will deliver tangible results, you must delve deep and keep gathering insights and key information. Experts are continuously learning. They never stop improving their skills. Ironically while they're probably the ones needing it the least, they're the ones studying the most.

So start becoming an expert in your field, too. Be curious about your goals. Learn as much as you can. Look for the best approaches and strategies. Identify areas in which you can improve. Never assume you're as good as you can be. Instead, demand more of yourself and you will inevitably become better and move closer to your goals.

Also, avoid making assumptions prematurely. During the process of alignment with reality, it is vital you keep experimenting and stay open-minded. When it comes to selling products or services, one of the biggest mistakes I see is when people project their way of thinking onto others. For example, these individuals may assume that because a certain marketing strategy won't work on them, it won't work on others. This is a dangerous assumption to make. The smarter way is to make as few assumptions as possible, remain curious and experiment with new ideas on a regular basis.

For example, when Amazon opened its ads platform in Germany, I started promoting my English-language books there immediately. I hoped to make an extra $50 to $100 per month. I didn't expect to make much since I have yet to translate any of my books into German. The first month I made around $1,000 in sales. Meanwhile, I saw writers in Facebook groups still wondering whether they should bother advertising their English-language books in Germany. The point is, we can all make poor assumptions. What we could do instead is to test. So rather than making assumptions, we should be running experiments.

- Think that person isn't into you? Go ask them.
- Think your boss will not give you a raise? Ask for one.
- Think your client will not pay you for additional services? Offer them additional services and see what happens.

Poor assumptions lead to ineffective actions (or no action at all) which generate poor results. Therefore never stop experimenting. Be open-minded and verify any assumptions you may hold by taking action and testing them.

* * *

Action step

Remain curious by engaging in the following activities:

- Stay up to date by checking out new publications on a regular basis.
- Identify the experts in your industry and follow them.
- Challenge your assumptions regularly and revise your strategy as necessary.

- See how you can apply ideas or strategies from areas that are unrelated to your goal.
- Look for trends and practice predicting what could happen in the coming years.

F. Listening to your emotions

Just because an answer is logical doesn't necessarily mean it's what you should be doing. Human beings tend to be more emotional than rational. More often than not, we make decisions based on *feelings* rather than *logic*.

Now why does it matter?

Because to achieve any goal in your life, you must ensure that you have strong emotional reasons for doing so. Logic itself will not be sufficient. For instance, you may find a wonderful business opportunity that could make you a lot of money. However, if you don't feel pulled toward it, you won't take the necessary action to succeed.

Beware of things that sound good on paper. Personally, I don't just look at the most profitable activity or what people around me tell me I should do. I focus on the activities I'm really excited about. If something excites me, I'll be able to stick to it for long enough to achieve results over time. On the other hand, if I choose to do something just for the financial reward or because it's what others tell me to do, I will likely give up before completion.

For example, a business consultant told one of my coaching clients, a film producer, to create TV commercials as a way to generate cash flow for his business. At the time, this made perfect sense since TV commercials pay well, and it wouldn't take him that much time to produce them. But guess what? As far as I know, my client never got around doing it. Why? Because he wasn't interested in making TV commercials.

The takeaway here is, you must take into consideration how you feel about a particular goal. You can have all the support you need and the best information out there, but if you aren't motivated, you will never achieve your goal and will only end up wasting your time and resources.

* * *

Action step

Using your action guide, answer the following questions:

- How motivated do you feel about your goal?
- What could you do to boost your motivation? Could you reframe your goal, find other reasons to incentivize yourself, or change it altogether?

In summary, to refine your model of reality you could:

1. Challenge your assumptions and identify what's really true and what is not.
2. Ask yourself smart questions that guide your thinking and boost your results.
3. Interview knowledgeable people in your field.
4. Find the highest quality information possible through extensive research.
5. Don't assume. Test, test, test. Be curious. Avoid making inaccurate assumptions.
6. Listen to your emotions. How you feel is more important than what you think you should do.

Remember, the more aligned you are with reality, the better results you're likely to obtain.

4

AVOIDING COMMON MISCONCEPTIONS AND DELUSIONAL THINKING

Are you really putting in all the effort required to achieve your goal, or do you merely think you are?

To attain ambitious goals, you must be willing to face reality. You should continuously attempt to align yourself with reality and ask yourself whether your strategy and level of action match your dream. Sadly, many people have misconceptions that prevent them from taking the actions required to achieve their goals. In this section, we'll go over four common ones.

- Misconception #1— I deserve to be successful.
- Misconception #2 — I do great work, therefore I should be successful.
- Misconception #3 — I'm just one breakthrough away from ...
- Misconception #4 — I'm already good enough and don't need to improve.

Misconception #1—I deserve to be successful

Many people have an entitlement mentality. These individuals believe they deserve an exciting job, great health and their fair share of happiness and success. Sometimes they also believe they should be rewarded in some capacity just because they care about a cause.

When I started self-publishing books, I was excited about the opportunity to help others by giving them practical tips and insights about personal development. I cared as much about my readers as the most successful indie writers in my field. Consequently, I deserved to make good money, right?

Wrong.

Just because we care about something doesn't mean we're entitled to anything. Sure, caring is the first step toward creating valuable products or services that could generate income in the mid-to-long term. But it's not enough. The second step is to take action and put in the time and energy required to reach our goal.

If we care about people and are truly committed to making a difference in the world, we should do whatever it takes. We must show the world we mean business. Just because we have noble intent doesn't mean we deserve success.

So how serious are you about reaching your goals? What are you willing to do to achieve them?

Misconception #2—I do great work therefore, I should be successful

Just because you produce high-quality work doesn't guarantee you'll be successful in your endeavors. There are many talented painters, gifted writers and singers, and brilliant inventors who will remain unknown for the rest of their lives.

A writer once complained her finance book didn't sell well. Yet, she was convinced it was better than *Rich Dad, Poor Dad*, the book ranked number in the field. The author, Robert T. Kiyosaki, told her he was a best-*selling* author, not a best-*writing* one. His book might not have been the best written one, but it was marketed effectively, allowing it to sell extremely well. The point is, doing great work is important, but it's often insufficient. You also need to promote your work effectively if you wish to have any impact.

Also, creating good work is not a one-time thing. You have to produce quality work consistently and repeatedly. For example, only a tiny minority of writers become successful with their first book, no matter how well-written it may be. But writers who release books consistently and promote them diligently can achieve success, even if their book is not the best out there.

Misconception #3—I'm just one breakthrough away from ...

After all these years of hard work, you're now one breakthrough away from "making it". Or are you?

The problem is, you've been in the same situation for years. For every new product, service or marketing campaign you launched, you thought you would finally get the recognition you deserve. But that long-awaited breakthrough never arrived.

Here is the truth. If you've been one breakthrough away from reaching your goal for too long, it's likely you're nowhere near success. Your breakthrough might not be coming any time soon (if ever). Don't get me wrong, patience and perseverance are critical. However, it doesn't mean that patience and perseverance will work in your current situation.

This is where it can get tricky. I believe the key to knowing whether you should keep going on the same path or not is to look at your situation as objectively as possible. To do so, ask yourself some of the following questions:

- What makes me believe that if I keep doing what I'm

doing I will eventually reach my goal? Where is the concrete evidence?

- How long have I been working on this particular goal? And why didn't I get the breakthrough I needed earlier?
- What tangible results have I achieved and what key milestones have I reached so far? How powerful are they in terms of indicating that I am on the right track and should keep going?
- Am I really putting in all the time and energy required to attain my goal? Am I doing what successful people in my field do? If not, what could I start doing now, or what could I do differently?

If you think you're close to having the breakthrough you've been waiting for, check that this is actually the case. Otherwise, you'll risk wasting even more time.

Misconception #4—I'm already good enough and don't need to improve

Thinking you're good at what you do doesn't mean it's actually the case. Perhaps you aren't as good as you think. When I started my blog in 2014, I thought my articles were great. When I read some of them a few years later, I was really disappointed. I could see so many issues that I was unable to identify at the time.

That's why you should always aim to improve. World-class performers, whether athletes, singers or actors, continuously strive to become better. Why shouldn't you? If your goal is that important to you, do the work needed to become the best you possibly can.

To summarize, most misconceptions are due to two main factors:

1. Arrogance/pride. We assume we deserve success and we

think we are better than others, or we believe we shouldn't have to work that hard.

2. Delusion. We have completely unrealistic expectations, and we fail to understand what it takes to reach our goals.

To get rid of these misconceptions, we must humble ourselves and be willing to learn from our mistakes. We must set our egos aside and listen to any feedback we receive. Then we must sharpen our thinking and take consistent action toward our goals, replace delusion with more realistic expectations and build the true confidence that comes from actual experience (see also the section, *How your ego affects your thinking*).

* * *

Action step

On a scale from 1 to 10 (1 being irrelevant and 10 being spot on), rate how each of these four misconceptions applies to your specific situation. Write down your answers in your action guide.

5

HOW TO CREATE AN EFFECTIVE PROCESS

Now that you have refined your model of reality, you must put in place an effective process to help you achieve your goal(s). An effective process is one that, when followed on a regular basis (often daily), leads you to reach your goals or at least to maximize your chance of success.

Here is a great question that may help you understand whether your process is accurate:

"If I keep doing what I'm doing today or this week, will I accomplish my goal?"

If your answer here is "no" or "I'm not sure", you might need to improve your process.

To implement an effective process, you must identify the key tasks that will enable you to move from where you are now to where you want to be in the future. Sometimes they are straightforward —for me, it's writing—sometimes they aren't.

In his book, *High Performance Habits*, Brendon Burchard talks about the "big five moves". His main argument is that there are usually five major projects or tasks that when completed successfully allow people to achieve their goal.

When he decided to be a New York Times best-selling author, Burchard interviewed several best-selling authors to identify what they did specifically. He then concluded that he should focus on the following tasks:

1. Finish writing a good book,
2. Self-publish or get an agent if you want a major publishing deal,
3. Start blogging and posting to social media and use these to build an email list,
4. Create a book promotion page and offer great bonuses to entice people to buy the book, and
5. Get five to ten people with a big email list to promote the book.

By focusing on these five big moves, he was able to make his book, *The Millionaire Messenger*, a New York Times bestseller.

Note that an effective process is different from an easy one. Some of your key moves may be simple while others may be really challenging. For instance, writing a good book is easier said than done. And finding five to ten influencers to promote your book can be incredibly difficult, especially if you're just getting started. However, knowing what to focus on will allow you to direct most of your time and energy toward activities that really count.

The bottom line is, for whatever goals you have, there are usually a few key tasks that will generate the desired tangible results. Your job is to find them and create an effective process around them.

* * *

Action step

Using your action guide, write down all the things you could do to achieve your goal. Don't censure or limit yourself. Just include everything that comes to mind. Try to produce at least ten to twenty actions.

A. Narrowing your options

You should now have a long list of actions you could take to reach your goal. The next step is to start eliminating the nonessential tasks so that only the most effective actions remain. To narrow your options, you need to establish a clear strategy. Having a strategy will help you determine your best plan of action and perhaps more importantly, it will also identify what you should *avoid* doing.

I. The importance of having a clear strategy

Many people fall prey to short-lived tactics and other gimmicks, jumping from one "sure thing" to the next, never achieving anything significant. For instance, they'll jump from one fad diet to next will abandon one training course for a new (seemingly) more exciting program or will give up on a challenging project to start a new one. This type of behavior is often referred to as the "Shiny Object Syndrome".

Generally speaking, the less clear your strategy is, the more likely you are to become distracted by new shiny objects, concepts or fads. To avoid this, it's critical you spend time creating a well-defined strategy that you genuinely believe will enable you to achieve your goals. The more you trust your strategy, the easier it will be to reject other approaches, no matter how promising they may appear.

a. Strategy vs. tactic

Many people fail to grasp the difference between a strategy and a tactic which is a serious issue. Let's briefly go over what strategies and tactics are.

Strategy: A strategy is a concerted plan designed to reach a long-term goal. It consists of a set of coordinated actions that (you hope) will lead you to achieve your goal. The key phrase here is "coordinated actions". You're not trying a bunch of random things hoping for the best. Each of your moves is part of a clear and effective strategy and, as such, you can explain to anybody why exactly you're undertaking a specific activity and how it fits into your overall strategy.

Tactic: A tactic is an action that is *part* of an overall strategy. It's only one of several actions your overall strategy consists of.

The problem occurs when you use tactics as if they were independent pieces you can pick and assemble together. In truth, a tactic in itself usually has little or no value. It's only relevant when combined with other tactics in a coordinated manner (i.e., as part of a sound, cohesive strategy).

For instance, one of my major goals is to become the number one self-help indie author on the entire Amazon US store. My current strategy to achieve that goal is to:

Release books every two months or so in the self-help niche and advertise them heavily using the Amazon ads platform with the intention of riding the Amazon algorithm in the mid-to-long term.

If I suddenly relied on tactics such as organizing seminars or shooting videos to sell more books, my actions would be out of alignment with my overall strategy. Here, to stick to my strategy, I need to write and publish books consistently and to optimize my ads.

Now you might wonder how I know my current strategy will allow me to become the number one self-help indie author.

Well I don't know for sure. However, my decision is based on the solid assumptions I've been refining over the past few years.

Let me share some of them to illustrate the importance of having good assumptions before establishing any long-term strategy.

Assumption #1: The Amazon algorithm will sell books for me

How I know this:

- I've read many books from established indie authors who have a decent grasp of the way the Amazon algorithm works.
- I've noticed a few indie authors have a couple of books that have been selling extremely well for several years. Because they don't have a huge platform, it's unlikely they heavily promote their books outside of the Amazon ecosystem (i.e., Amazon is indeed doing the heavy lifting for them and if it works for other authors, why wouldn't it work for me?).
- I now have a few books that have been selling consistently for months which tends to confirm that assumption.

Assumption #2: The more books, the better

How I know this:

Most successful indie writers (whether fiction or nonfiction), argue that the best marketing tool for an author is to publish another book, many of them having written dozens of their own. I believe this is key since there is some luck involved in the success of any book. Consequently, the more books I publish, the more likely I am to have a winner. In addition, the more books I write, the better I become at writing which increases the likelihood my readers will enjoy my books and recommend them to others.

For instance, I only started seeing decent sales after publishing my seventh book. And my ninth book, *Master Your Emotions*, has been very popular on Amazon. It was even picked up by several foreign publishers.

Of course, writing more books is not necessarily the best solution. It all depends on your strategy. Some people will use their book to promote their products and services, making a lot of money on the backend. This is fine, too. It's just a different strategy.

Assumption #3: I have what it takes

How I know this:

- I've received enough positive feedback and have made enough sales to *know* my goal is achievable.
- In the past, I've written good quality books within two months or so. Therefore, I know I can repeat the process.
- I've developed the mindset required to hit my goal, and I firmly believe I have enough self-discipline and resourcefulness to be successful. As proof, I worked on my business twenty to thirty hours a week for over a year while holding down a full-time job.

The assumptions described above led me to believe that my goal was realistic (although not easy) and my strategy is sound.

What about you? Do you have a clear strategy consisting of well-coordinated tactics, or do you rely on ninja tricks and short-lived gimmicks? And how do you know your strategy is sound? What assumptions is it based on and what evidence do you have that these assumptions are accurate?

b. Your strategy determines what *not* to do

Having a clear strategy also means identifying what you should *not* do. For example, if I did everything under the sun to boost my sales, it would mean I had no defined strategy. Once I've established a specific strategy, I avoid doing anything that doesn't fit into it. For instance, here is what I decided *not* to do (except in rare cases):

- Use social media (Facebook, Pinterest, LinkedIn, et cetera) to promote my books.
- Go on podcasts.
- Record YouTube videos.
- Organize seminars.
- Run webinars.
- Write blog posts.
- Get traditionally published.
- Get my books into libraries.

Now to implement my strategy successfully, I also need to rely on a variety of tactics. For these tactics to work, they must be part of my overall strategy. For example, there is nothing wrong with doing podcast interviews, writing blog posts or tweeting daily. However, none of these activities fit into my strategy of writing and releasing books consistently. As such, I have decided they should be avoided.

The bottom line is, to achieve tangible results, you must focus on a few activities for a long enough period of time. The same way you can't cut down a tree by hitting different spots with each ax swing, you can't make significant progress by using unrelated tactics one after another. Yet this is what many people do. They spread themselves too thin, doing way too many things. This lack of focus prevents them from having major breakthroughs in their lives and in their businesses. If you don't have a well-defined strategy, the same thing will probably happen to you, too.

As an illustration of this, a short while ago I was listening to a webinar run by an experienced book marketer. I felt completely overwhelmed just listening to the sheer number of things I was supposed to do if I wanted to be successful. She suggested I should:

- Create a blog and update it consistently,
- Publish guest posts on other people's blogs,
- Build an email list,
- Create book trailers and post them on YouTube,
- Go to events,
- Set up webinars,
- Host Facebook Lives,
- Connect with influencers,
- Run ads (Amazon, Facebook, BookBub, et cetera),
- Develop a presence on Facebook, Twitter, Instagram, Pinterest et cetera,
- Get more reviews,
- Get my books into bookstores and libraries, and
- Send out press releases.

If you were an aspiring writer, wouldn't you feel overwhelmed?

Then she proceeded to tell the audience that they could hire her if they needed help. Of course, they needed help! How could they possibly manage to do all these things by themselves?

Now the interesting part is, I'm a full-time writer and do precious few of these things. In fact, I:

- Barely post on social media,
- Seldom blog,
- Almost never go on podcasts,
- Don't do Facebook Lives or record videos,
- Never send press releases,

- Don't try to get my books into libraries,
- Never organize events, and
- I never run webinars or seminars.

I simply write more books, run ads, build my email list and, occasionally, connect with a few writers. And I know other successful indie writers in my field who do the same. Now it doesn't mean other activities won't work, it just means they must be part of a long-term strategy.

What about you? What strategy do you think would work best for you? What things should you *not* do?

If you want to learn how to get rid of the Shiny Object Syndrome and stop spreading yourself too thin, refer to the third book in this series, *Master Your Focus*.

* * *

Action step

Using your action guide, complete the following exercises:

- Review the ideas you came up with in the previous exercise.
- Come up with at least three possible strategies by combining some of your ideas in a coherent way.
- For each strategy, take a moment to think of all the things this strategy suggests you should *not* be doing.

B. Putting in place an effective process

i. Process goals vs. outcome goals

It is easy to become obsessed by results. However, you don't have one hundred percent control over the outcome of any of your goals. You cannot be certain you will make a specific sum of money, sell a certain number of products or lose a set amount of weight. However, what you can do is put a specific process in place to improve your chances of success. For instance, I cannot be sure that I will sell 100,000 books in 2020 (outcome goal), but I can:

- Release six books and two boxsets,
- Translate three books or more in Spanish, German and French, and
- Spend ten hours a week optimizing my ads.

All the above goals are process goals. As such, I have absolute control over them. I believe achieving them (among other things) will support my overall outcome goal of selling 100,000 books this year.

Process goals help remove uncertainty and release self-imposed pressure coming from focusing solely on the outcome. To achieve any outcome goal, all you can ever do is:

- Identify the most effective process possible,
- Set process goals that will help you achieve your outcome goals,
- Create daily habits related to your goal,
- Stay consistent over the long term until you reach your goal, and
- Refine your process when necessary based on the feedback you receive.

Now you won't always hit your goals, but if you develop an effective process and implement a solid daily routine, you will inevitably make progress toward them.

To sum up, set a direction by having a very specific outcome goal (e.g., making $100,000, writing six books, losing twenty pounds, et cetera), then implement a process to maximize your chance for success. Finally, spend most of your time and energy focusing on the process. Don't let the lack of short-term results affect you. Stick to the process, remain consistent, and you'll put yourself in the best possible place to make significant progress.

For instance, processes could be things such as:

- Writing for forty-five minutes every morning,
- Cold-calling five prospects every day,
- Replacing sugary drinks with water during your meals, or
- Going to the gym three times a week.

Once you have determined the effective process for your goals, make sure you stick with your strategy. Make sure you evaluate your progress based on how well you're sticking to the process, *not* based on the short-term results you attain.

When necessary, refine your process to confirm its effectiveness. For instance, you may need to spend more time writing every day. Or you may discover that calling five prospects isn't enough to hit your target. As a result, you might choose to increase the number of cold calls or adjust your long-term goal.

Action step

Complete the exercise below, referring to your action guide:

- Review the strategies you've already identified and select the one you believe to be the best.
- Write down the process you think you need to implement to make that strategy work (e.g., what you need to do

every day/regularly to maximize your chances for success).

C. Cultivating long-term thinking

Humans aren't wired to think long term. If anything, we're designed to give more importance to the short term which is why many of us have such a hard time delaying gratification. Perhaps you recognize yourself in one of the following situations:

- You spend all your money, despite knowing you should save for a rainy day.
- You keep eating unhealthy food, despite knowing you should take better care of your health.
- You binge-watch Netflix programs until the middle of the night, knowing you should go to bed.

To develop an accurate model of reality, you must change your relationship with time and actively work on overcoming your biases and natural tendencies.

1. Why thinking long term is critical

One of the laws I discuss in my book *Success is Inevitable*, is the "Law of Long-Term Thinking". I believe this is one of the most important laws when it comes to success. People who can delay gratification and think long term will almost always be more successful in the long run than people who can't. Having a long-term perspective, these individuals adopt a better overall strategy for their life and make wiser decisions. For example, they might save more money, invest in their own education or eat healthier food than they otherwise would.

However as human beings, we often fail to embrace patience and reap all the benefits that come with it, which brings us to our next point.

2. The value of patience

Most of us struggle to understand how long-term thinking works and why it's so powerful. We overestimate what we can do in one year, but underestimate what we can do in five or ten years. We are caught up in short-term thinking and consider our most ambitious goals as impossible. Seeing only the obstacles ahead of us, we feel discouraged or even powerless.

Interestingly, the younger we are, the more distorted our perception of time tends to be. Take teenagers, for instance. They have decades ahead of them, yet they want everything right away. They resent their parents for not letting them go out, or they can't wait to reach the age of maturity so that they can drive a car and become independent.

This chronic lack of perspective does not just apply to teenagers though. It applies to everyone. Today, a forty-year-old person has, on average, quite a few more decades to live. That's a lot of time, but how often do such people feel as though it's already too late, that they don't have enough time?

Here is the good news. You don't need twenty years to transform your life. You can make drastic changes in just a few years. So even if you happen to be in your fifties, sixties or even seventies, you still have time. If you were truly committed to making changes in your life, imagine where you could be in just three to five years, let alone a decade or more.

3. The trap of unrealistic expectations

Many people have unrealistic expectations. This is especially true when they start a new venture. It was certainly the case when I started out. When I started a blog a few years ago, I thought it would be a big success. Every time I published an article I thought, "This is it! People are going to love it. This one's going viral."

It never happened.

The bottom line is, when you start something, you have no idea what you don't know. Often, you fail to realize exactly what it takes to be successful. This may lead you to give up prematurely when you don't see the results you think you deserve. You may even believe something is wrong with you. This false concept is reinforced by all the so-called gurus who promise quick results with the minimum of effort.

No. Nothing is wrong with you. If you're struggling, that's probably because it's part of the process. Fortunately, they are many things you can do to improve your results. However, you still need to follow a specific process and do the work—there is no way around it.

A short while ago, I came across a sales pitch that made me cringe. It was one of those pitches written by expert copywriters who are selling you the dream that you can make tons of money without doing much work. The main message was that you can make $10,000 a month in "passive" income by writing short books. Just one book written over the weekend could potentially make you $10,000 per month for years to come. Yes, that's right, you read that correctly. Amazing, isn't it? I wonder why I've bothered spending years writing books when all I needed to do was to write a few short books over the weekend.

This is a perfect example of someone pitching you a terrible model of reality that will never lead you to any tangible positive results. If you buy into this idea that you can make $10,000 a month from publishing a few short books, you will start thinking something is wrong with you when you fail to achieve the results you were promised.

Now you will inevitably have unrealistic expectations as you get started, but the key is to:

- Maintain a long-term focus,
- Continuously refine your model of reality, and
- Stick to your process day after day, even in the absence of immediate results.

4. Why worthy goals take time and effort

Patience is critical because to achieve any worthy goal requires a great deal of time and effort. In fact, this is how you know a goal is worth pursuing in the first place. You can't expect to design your dream career, build fulfilling relationships or become financially independent without putting in the work, can you? So if it's hard and progress is slow, that's okay. In most cases, this is how it should be.

I credit a large part of my success as an indie author to my ability to think long term. In my first book, *Goal Setting* published in 2015, I wrote that I wanted to become one of the best known personal development experts in the world. At the time, I had no network, no followers and no prior experience of writing books. I wasn't even writing in my mother tongue! However, I *was* willing to work hard and spend as many years as necessary to achieve my goal. As I'm writing this book, I've sold close to 100,000 copies of my books and signed foreign deals with Russian, Brazilian, Vietnamese, Indian and Japanese publishers. I think it's a good start. But it certainly didn't happen overnight. It took me three years before I started making money from my writing.

Note that any major life-changing goals will probably take three to five years to achieve (and sometimes more). Therefore, if you really want to achieve something important and significant, give yourself ample time to make it happen. Think long term. Life is a marathon, not a sprint. You have more time than you think. If you keep moving forward, putting one foot after the other every day, you'll find yourself accomplishing far more than you could ever imagine.

The point is, don't let short-termism distort your reality and make you feel as though you don't have enough time. Do the work every day and let the magic of "compounding" work in your favor. The more consistent you can be, the more momentum you'll build and the more impressive your results will be over time.

To learn in greater detail how to build momentum and sustain motivation long term, refer to the second book in this series, *Master Your Motivation*.

* * *

Action step

Using your action guide, complete the sentence below with as many answers as you can think of:

If I was better at thinking long term, I would ...

5. How to transition from short-term to long-term thinking

While some people may be better than others at thinking long term, I believe long-term thinking is a skill anyone can acquire. In this section, we'll discuss six specific things you can do to develop that skill. These things are:

- Creating a long-term vision.
- Thinking of your long-term goals often.
- Dedicating time to focus on the big picture.
- Learning to love the process.
- Letting go of the fear of missing out.
- Reminding yourself to be patient.

a. Creating a long-term vision

Clearly, the first step to becoming better at projecting yourself into the future is to create a long-term vision. It's difficult, if not impossible, to think in the long term without having a long-term vision to strive for. Without a clear vision, you risk doing "busywork" that will often be out of alignment with your goals. You need to make sure that the things you work on today are moving you closer to your ultimate vision.

* * *

Action step

Think of a major goal. Then using your action guide, answer the following questions:

- What's the ultimate vision behind your goal?
- How can you make this goal even more specific?
- Why is this goal so important to you?
- What financial, physical, mental and/or emotional benefits will you gain from reaching it?

b. Thinking of your long-term goals often

Once you have established a long-term goal, you need to look at it on a regular basis. To do so you can:

- Create a vision board and put it somewhere you'll see it often,
- Write down your long-term goal on a piece of paper and put it on your desk or somewhere you'll be able to see it daily, and/or
- Read your long-term goal every day/week.

The more often you think about your long-term goals, the better you'll become at adopting a long-term vision.

c. Dedicating time to focus on the big picture

To ensure you stay focused on your long-term vision, I invite you to carve out some time during your week to zoom out and think in terms of the overall picture. For instance, you could dedicate thirty-to-sixty minutes every Sunday to assess your progress and ensure you're heading in the right direction. During this time, you can ask yourself the following questions:

- What am I satisfied with?
- What do I want or need to improve?
- What can I do differently to speed up my progress?
- If I were to start the week all over again, what would I do differently?
- If I keep doing what I've done this week, will I achieve my long-term goal? If not, what changes do I need to make?
- Is my current strategy the best one possible? If not, how can I refine it to make it even better?
- What are the very few things that generate most of my results? Can I focus more on these things?
- What are all the things that haven't proven to be effective so far? Can I get rid of some of them?
- If I only work on one thing this week/month/year, what would be best in terms of overall progress?

Having this kind of weekly strategic session will ensure you spend time thinking of your future and avoid getting caught up in the day-to-day chaos life can sometimes become.

Action step

Carve out time every week to focus on the big picture. To help you do so, go through the list of questions above (you'll also find them in your action guide).

d. Learning to love the process

While we all want positive outcomes, obsessing over the results isn't the most effective strategy. Optimal results don't magically appear instantly. They are generated through processes. Therefore, the key to becoming a long-term thinker is to focus on the process and learn to love it and respect it.

We often buy into the myth that one day, when we finally achieve our goals, we'll live happily ever after. However, that's not the way the human brain works. We tend to be at our happiest when we pursue worthy goals. This is why as soon as we reach a goal, we feel the need to set a new and even more exciting target. This means that most of your happiness occurs during the process leading to the achievement of your goals. As such, obsessing over the results is missing the point. The joy you experience once you reach any goal will only be short-lived. The process *is* the real goal. The journey is all there is. For that reason, enjoying the process is the best way to be happy while making progress toward your most important goals.

* * *

Action step

Complete the sentence below using your action guide:

For me, focusing more on the process would mean ...

e. Letting go of the fear of missing out

Many people are afraid of missing out on life. They live in constant fear of missing that one party, opportunity or person. For instance:

- When they can't attend a party, they become anxious.

What if something amazing happens and they aren't able to see it?

- When they travel, they try to see as many things as possible, packing their days with more visits than they can handle. They spend hours researching for fear of missing the one thing they should absolutely see.
- When they miss the opportunity to date someone they really liked, they feel discouraged, wondering if they will ever meet such a wonderful person again.

Ultimately, the fear of missing out is the manifestation of a scarcity mindset. It results from a lack of trust in the world and in its ability to provide more opportunities than you can imagine. Perhaps, even more importantly, it is the manifestation of a lack of trust in yourself and in your capacity to create wonderful memories. In reality, there is no shortage of enjoyable experiences. There is no limit to the number of great memories you can generate.

When you fear missing out, you'll tend to be more easily distracted by new opportunities. This is why it's important you learn to control that fear better. People who fall for the Shiny Object Syndrome are usually scared of missing out. They believe there is a magic pill out there, and they can't stop themselves from searching for it.

Conversely, long-term thinkers understand this is an inaccurate way of living. They know they need to craft a sound strategy, refine it over time and stick to it for the long term. They know that to succeed they will have to "miss out" on a lot of things. This is actually what having a strategy is all about: being able to say "no" to everything that isn't part of the overall strategy. Remember, if you don't say "no" to requests that eat into your valuable time, it means you don't have a real strategy.

Action step

Complete the exercises below using your action guide:

- Write down the area(s) of your life in which you experience fear of missing out.
- Select one specific area or goal and write down all the opportunities that actually exist out there. What are your options? What could you do about it?
- Take a moment to appreciate all the opportunities available to you.

f. Reminding yourself to be patient

For most people, being a long-term thinker doesn't come naturally. To enhance your ability to think long term, you must remind yourself of the importance of remaining patient. Remember, you're biased to want things immediately, but you may need to hang fire a little.

People think I'm naturally patient. I'm *not*. In fact, I'm extraordinarily *impatient*. I want things to happen and to happen now. But at the same time, I deeply appreciate the value of patience. I understand that any meaningful goal requires months or years of work and that with enough patience, I can achieve almost anything I want. This is why I constantly remind myself to be patient, and I believe you should, too.

* * *

Action step

Regularly remind yourself that you have time. To do this, you can:

- Create your own mantras such as "life is a marathon, not a sprint", or simply "I have time" or "be patient". Then think of them often, write them down and/or display them on your desk or on your wall.
- Watch Gary Vee's videos, "Overnight Success" and "People have forgotten the art of patience" on Youtube).
- Visualize everything you've already done in the past few months/years and remind yourself of how much more time you have available to achieve even greater things.

6. Increasing the value you give to time

Time is one of the most valuable assets you have. Yet, you may fail to use it as effectively as possible. If you're serious about achieving tangible results, you must learn to increase the value you assign to your time. An effective way to do this is to change how you set goals.

The way you set goals affects your perception of time. For instance, if you don't set goals, there will be no deadline to hit and therefore, no sense of urgency. If you set yearly goals, your deadlines may be months away which will minimize your sense of urgency. Alternatively, if you set thirty-day or ninety-day goals, you will instill a real sense of urgency.

In their book, *The 12-Week Year: Get More Done in 12 Weeks Than Others do in 12 Months*, the authors, Brian P. Moran and Michael Pennington, suggest we should change the way we perceive time and consider the ninety-day period in front of us as if it were an entire year. That is, when setting goals, we should think in ninety-day periods and do away with annual goals. Imagine if you needed to achieve your yearly goals in ninety days? What would you do differently? Would you still procrastinate? Would you still take it easy, thinking you had plenty of time?

Thinking in ninety-day segments will make time much more real to you. Your goals will feel more concrete. You'll be able to see the finish line from the very beginning which will inspire you to take action right away. As a result, each and every upcoming day will become much more important and valuable.

So instead of thinking in terms of years, start thinking in ninety-day periods and make sure you progress toward your goals each day.

In *Part III. Empowering your model of reality*, we'll see how to break down your goals to boost your productivity.

a. Be impatient short term but patient long term

At first glance, the concept of striving for both patience *and* urgency at the same time might appear paradoxical. However, let me explain why I think this is not the case.

Whereas you must be patient over the long term knowing that you will not always achieve tangible results as fast as you'd like, you must be impatient in the short term by having specific goals and firm deadlines that feel very real to you. By doing this, you'll be nudged to move toward your goals every single day. By focusing on the process with a sense of urgency and by remaining patient month after month, you'll eventually achieve your long-term goals.

So learn to be *impatient* in the short term, but *patient* over the long term.

b. Busy vs. productive

To increase the value of time, you must replace "busy" work with "productive" work. This begins by becoming more aware of everything you do. Before you start any task, ask yourself why you're doing it and what exactly you're trying to achieve. As you do this, you might realize you don't need to complete the task at all.

As I said earlier, while building my online business, I used to perform so many different work tasks. I posted daily on Facebook, shot YouTube videos, uploaded images on Pinterest, wrote guest posts, blogged, et cetera. But over time and as I refined my model of reality, I started asking myself which of these things, if any, were useful. One day I stopped doing them, and I ended up reducing my workload by half almost overnight. These days, I'm very strategic in the way I work. Whenever I start feeling overwhelmed, I take it as a sign I'm doing things I probably shouldn't be attempting. As a result, I stop and think, and I modify my schedule accordingly.

You need to leverage the power of the 80/20 Principle. Remember that, roughly speaking, twenty percent of what you do will generate eighty percent of the results you obtain. Also, understand there is an opportunity cost behind everything you do. Whenever you choose to do one thing, you say no to everything else you could be doing instead.

For instance, being French, I thought that maybe I should translate some of my English-language books into French myself. However, after due consideration, I realized it didn't make sense for the following reasons:

- I'm not a good translator.
- I don't particularly enjoy doing translation work.
- I could write a new book in English instead, which could be a much more lucrative activity while reaching a newer audience with additional content.

In short, aligning yourself with reality also means doing what's most important while eliminating the rest. Less is often more.

7-step method to approach any new task

To make sure you're as productive as possible, I encourage you to follow the 7-step process outlined below before you start any significant task.

Step 1. Prioritizing your task

Before you start working on a task, ask yourself:

- If I could do only one thing today, which task would have the most impact?
- Is this task moving me closer to my main goal?
- Do I really need to do it right now, or can I do it later?

Train yourself to think in terms of priorities and keep an eye on the big picture.

Step 2. Assessing the validity of your task

To ensure the task is something you actually need to do, ask yourself the following questions:

- Do I really need to do this task?
- Is right now the best time? What would happen if I delay it for a week? A month? Forever?
- Do I need to do this task, or am I doing it because it makes me feel good? In short, am I working on this task to escape from what I really should be doing?

There is nothing more unproductive than doing something you didn't need to do in the first place. Answering the above questions can help you avoid making such a mistake.

Step 3. Clarifying what needs to be done

Before working on a task, be certain you know exactly what is required. Therefore, before starting any task, ask yourself:

- What exactly do I need to do here?
- What am I trying to accomplish?
- What does the finished product look like?

Be specific. By knowing exactly what the output needs to be, you'll be able to optimize your approach and tackle the task more effectively.

Step 4. Determining whether you should be the person doing it

You have strengths, but you also have weaknesses. Whenever possible, try to delegate any task someone else can do better, faster or more cheaply than you. Ask yourself the following questions:

- Is this task really worthy of my time?
- Can someone else do it better than me? If so, can I ask for help?
- What would happen if I simply remove/postpone this task?
- Do I enjoy working on this task? Does it motivate me?

Little by little, you want to get into the habit of outsourcing everything you're not good at and focus only on the high-value tasks at which you excel.

Step 5. Finding out the most effective way to tackle a task

Just taking a few minutes to work out the best way to approach a task can save you so much time. Ask yourself the following questions:

- What tool(s) can I use, people can I ask or method can I

rely on to complete this task as efficiently and effectively as possible?

- What skill(s) could I learn or improve to help me complete this task faster in the future?

Step 6. Batching the task with other similar tasks

Some jobs can be combined with other tasks that require the same type of effort or preparation. For instance, many YouTubers block one full day a week to record videos as opposed to creating one video every day.

Ask yourself:

- Can I batch this task with other similar tasks to boost my productivity?

Step 7. Automating/systemizing your task

Finally, you want to find ways to automate or systemize your task, especially if it's a repetitive one. Ask yourself:

- Can I create templates to reuse every time I work on this or on similar tasks? For instance, you could design templates for the specific emails, presentations or documents you need to create over and over.
- Can I create a checklist? Checklists provide you with specific steps to follow, making it less likely you will become distracted or confused.

By following this 7-step approach you can boost your productivity significantly. Even though it may take time for you to internalize this process, once you do, it will become almost automatic.

So far, we have discussed what you can do to align yourself with reality and achieve better results. Now it's time to see how you can put your new model of reality to use in a way that maximizes your odds of success long term. It's time to empower your model of reality.

* * *

Action step

Before starting any major or complex new task, go over the 7-step method to approach any task the right way. You'll also find it in your action guide.

PART III

EMPOWERING YOUR MODEL OF REALITY

Now that you have a better idea of how to think accurately and put in place effective processes, it's time to make sure your model of reality works for you in the real world.

We have all met people who seem to know everything about the theory, but have little to no results to show for their efforts. To avoid becoming one of these people, you must ensure your actions are not only congruent with your new model of reality, but they also reinforce it. To do so, you must remove mental blocks and develop unshakeable self-confidence so that you truly believe in your ability to achieve your goals.

In this section, you'll discover how to design an empowering environment, adopt powerful beliefs, develop rock-solid confidence and expand your field of possibilities. Doing so will enable you to dramatically enhance the odds you will achieve your goals in any area of your life.

So are you ready to empower your model of reality and generate positive results? Let's get started.

1

DESIGN AN EMPOWERING ENVIRONMENT

Your environment has an enormous impact on the way you feel and the actions you take. When your environment is working against you, it is difficult to adopt a positive mindset and take the actions required to achieve your goals. For example, if people are casting doubts about your ability to succeed, you'll find it difficult to believe in or work toward any dream.

Therefore, to design the reality you want, you must surround yourself with positive people who will bring the best out of you. You must also ensure your environment facilitates the new behaviors and habits you want to adopt. You can change your environment by:

- Changing your peer group.
- Changing your physical environment.
- Optimizing your digital environment.

Let's explore each of these options.

A. Changing your peer group

It's said that we are the average of the five people we spend the most time with. Who are these five people for you? If you keep your current circle of friends, how likely are you to achieve your biggest dreams?

You'll tend to pick up the attitudes, habits and ways of thinking of people around you. To a certain extent, we can say that people you hang out with dictate how you think, feel and act. For this reason, you'll seldom—if ever—see successful people hanging out with negative or unsuccessful people any more than they absolutely have to.

Remember, whatever your goals or dreams, reaching them won't be easy. You'll need all the support you can gather, and this should start by surrounding yourself with the right people.

Action step

Using your action guide, answer the following questions:

- Who do I want to spend more time with?
- Who do I want to spend less time with?
- Which people have already achieved the goals I seek to achieve?
- Where can I find these positive and supportive people?

1. How to protect yourself from negative people

As you develop a new model of reality to reach your goals, you'll encounter naysayers and other dream killers. Although it is to be expected, it doesn't mean you should give them permission to influence your model of reality. These people have their own vision of the world and that's fine, but don't let them get into your head, drag you down and mess with your dreams. Instead, strengthen your model of reality by improving your peer group and building rock-solid confidence in yourself and in your vision. We'll see how to do that in great detail in the next section, *Developing unshakeable confidence*.

The truth is, in any interaction between you and another person, two realities clash. If you lack confidence and conviction, you're more likely to be sucked into the other person's version of "reality". This means you will allow their model of reality (i.e., their assumptions) to influence yours. For instance, if you lack confidence and they expect you to fail, it may lead you to reconsider your goals. If they say your art, book or product sucks, you may decide to give up. On the other hand, if they believe in you and offer encouragement, you'll feel great about yourself and become more optimistic.

This is why you must learn to develop more confidence and distance yourself from negative people. Over time and as you gain confidence, you'll be less affected by other people's opinions. Even so, there is no reason to hang out with naysayers any longer than you absolutely have to, right?

Now let's look at a few steps you can take to deal more effectively with negative people. You can:

- Ask for their support,
- Reduce the time you spend with them, and/or
- Refrain from sharing your goals with them.

a. Ask for their support

The first thing you can do is to ask them to support you. To do so, tell them exactly what you're trying to accomplish and why it's important to you. Then tell them why their help is so important and how much it would mean for you to have their full support.

In an ideal world, your friends and family will support you and want the best for you, but that's not always the way things work. If after talking with unsupportive people in your life, you notice no change in their attitude, try spending less time with them.

b. Reduce the time you spend with them

It's best not to spend all day around negative people. If you notice someone is dragging you down, take specific measures to distance yourself from that person. For instance, you can decide to meet him or her only once a week instead of two or three times a week. You can also decline invitations more often. By doing so, this toxic relationship may naturally die off over time.

c. Stop sharing your goals with them

Another step you can take to protect yourself from negative people is to avoid sharing your goals with them. If you feel they won't support you, just keep your goals for yourself and only share them with people who will encourage you. Repeatedly being told that you will fail with your new venture, never land your dream job or struggle to get your book published is a real downer. Cherish your dreams and only share them with people who deserve to know about them—people who have your best interests at heart.

Now what about the people you live with? How should you deal with them? Here are a few tips you can try.

Ask for their input/advice. The first thing you can try is to ask for their input. Ask them what they would do if they were in your shoes? For instance, how would they go about changing careers? What would they do if they needed to retire ten years early?

Further include them in your dream. If your goal or dream is something you believe they can benefit from as well, sell them on it. But instead of persuading them yourself, ask them how their life would be better once you reach that goal. In short, let them sell themselves on your goal. For instance, let's say you want to retire early by saving aggressively and investing your money. Your partner might not be on board with your plan at first. However, you could ask them to imagine what they would be doing if they could retire earlier than sixty-five. You could ask what would excite them most about early retirement. Once they have clear and exciting goals themselves, they may change their mind about your idea and start helping you progress towards your goal.

Get early results. Another option is to generate tangible results to show to your spouse, kids and/or parents. A couple of years ago, I received an email from one of my readers who loved my goal setting book and wanted his spouse to read it. However, she wasn't too keen on the idea. I suggested the best thing he could do was to start achieving goals and as he did so, she might feel inspired and pick up the book, too. It's easier to change others by becoming a role model than by issuing instructions. Most people don't like to be told what to do.

If none of these suggestions work, you might have to pursue your goals without their support. If they're actively against your goal, you have two options—either give up on your goal or carry on regardless of the consequences it may have on your relationship.

2. Surround yourself with people who will support you

One of the most effective ways to change how you think, feel and act is to change the people you hang out with. You need to be around positive and successful people who will push you to become your best self and who demand more of you. Here are a few things you can do to be around such positive people:

- Join groups of like-minded people.
- Create your own event.

- Look for a mentor.
- Hire a coach.

a. Join groups of like-minded people

To strengthen your model of reality, you need to surround yourself with people who are on the same path and, if possible, ahead of you. For instance, if you're an entrepreneur, you might want to join a group of entrepreneurs. If you are an aspiring writer, you might join Facebook groups dedicated to writers or attend author conferences.

Don't hesitate to contact people who are on the same path as you. The people who helped me the most are people I contacted myself. So be proactive. Even a few encounters can make a major difference in your life.

What group or groups could you join? Who could you contact?

b. Create your own event

If you can't find your tribe, why not create an event that will attract people you want to be surrounded with? For instance, last year I created a mastermind group with two other authors. The group has allowed us to share tips and strategies and has helped each of us achieve better results.

What about you? Who do you want to attract into your life and what kind of event could you organize that would appeal to them?

c. Look for a mentor

Having a mentor is one of the most effective ways to skyrocket your success. A great mentor will:

- Help you shift your mindset,
- Tell you what to do (and not to do), saving you months or years of work,

- Ask you smart questions and offer guidance, and
- Open their network to you (potentially).

However, finding the right mentor can be challenging. The more successful a person is, the busier they are—and the harder it will be to reach them.

There is no magic way to find a mentor, but there are a few things you can do to help get you started. The most important thing is to put yourself in the shoes of a potential future mentor. You need to think as he or she thinks. For instance, if I were to mentor someone, the main question I would ask myself is how committed that potential mentee is. I don't want to waste my time with someone who will disappear in a few months.

The bottom line is, you must be a good investment for your mentor. Many successful people are happy to share their knowledge and wisdom, but they want to make sure it will be worth their time. Bear this in mind when you look for a teacher. If you work hard on yourself first and aim to add value to your mentor, maybe they will decide to work with you.

Don't worry if you can't find a mentor. You can always have virtual mentors by reading books, buying courses or watching videos.

d. Hire a coach

Another way to find support and make tangible progress toward your goals is to work with a coach. By investing your hard-earned money in a coach, you'll also have skin in the game, making it more likely you'll take action and generate results.

Action step

Answer the questions below using your action guide:

- What group or groups could you join? Who could you contact?
- Who do you want to attract into your life and what kind of event could you organize that would appeal to them?
- Who would be the ideal mentor/coach for you?
- What one thing could you do to spend more time with people who will support your goal?

B. Change your physical environment

Is your physical environment inspiring you to perform at your best, or is it holding you back?

When it comes to your productivity and your ability to achieve tangible results, your physical environment plays an important part. In this section, we'll review a few things you can do to optimize it.

1. Declutter your environment

If you feel stuck right now and lack motivation, it might be a good idea to start decluttering your environment. For instance, you can begin with your desk whether at work or at home.

2. Make your goals visible

You should focus on your major goals as often as possible. The more you think about your goals, the more your subconscious will look for ways to make them a reality. And remember, your subconscious works 24/7.

To think about your goals more often, put them somewhere you can see them every day. For example, you could list them and attach the list to your wall. Alternatively, you could write them in a notebook and check it every day. You could also create a vision board with pictures representing each of your goals. The more often you look at your goals, the better. Doing so will prevent you from getting distracted and ensure you spend most of your time working on the things that truly matter to you.

Successful people think about their goals regularly throughout their day. They may even obsess over them. Why don't you?

3. Remove friction

How much junk food would you eat if you had an unlimited supply on your desk every day? Now imagine if you had to go to the supermarket every time you fancied some junk food. You'd probably eat less of it, right?

You want to make your core tasks and desired behaviors as easy as possible to perform each day. The less mental and physical effort required to start working on a task or adopting a certain behavior, the more likely you are to do it.

For example, if you want to write every morning, make sure you can access the files you need easily. Personally, I like to remove everything from my desk to avoid distractions. No cellphone. No food. No documents. Nothing. I might also turn off the Wi-Fi when necessary.

Check out the examples below:

- If you want to go for a run in the morning, prepare your running gear beforehand and make sure you can access it easily.
- If you have a creative job, you might want to keep a pen and paper in every room in case you need to capture a thought or idea.
- If your tasks involve spending a lot of time on the computer, make sure the files you need are well-organized and create a system that allows you to save any information that could be useful.

The bottom line is, designing an effective structure can provide long-term support for your goal. The better you optimize your environment, the easier it will be to maintain your daily habits and avoid distractions and procrastination.

For these reasons, you should constantly strive to implement things that have the potential to simplify your life, increase your day-to-day focus, and support your goal.

* * *

Action step

Using your action guide, spend a few minutes answering the following questions:

- What one thing could you do to spend more time with people who will support your goal? Example: I will spend less time with my negative friends.
- What one thing could you do to create a more positive environment to motivate yourself to work on your goal? Example: I will spend ten minutes every day reading inspirational materials.
- What one thing could you do to optimize your current environment and make it easier to work on your goal? Example: To avoid any distraction, I will remove everything from my desk when I work.

C. Optimizing your digital environment

How often do you check your emails? How much time do you spend on social media?

Distraction kills productivity. If you want to become highly productive and achieve most of your goals in the long term, you must eliminate as many distractions as possible to help you *focus*. Aim for zero distraction.

When applicable, I encourage you to:

- Turn off phone notifications.
- Turn off Wi-Fi (unless you really need internet access).
- Remove any unnecessary items from your desk or work environment.

Then get on with the work!

Here are some other things you might want to try:

- Install software to remove your Facebook newsfeed (e.g., the Chrome extension News Feed Eradicator for Facebook).
- Install browser extensions to remove recommendations on YouTube (e.g., the Chrome extension DF Tube).
- Install apps that temporarily limit access to websites such as Facebook, YouTube or any sites you visit more often than you should (e.g., the app Freedom).

Emails can also be a huge source of distraction. I invite you to unsubscribe from any newsletters not closely related to your most important goals or projects. You can always re-subscribe later.

The less time you spend on social media/emails, the more proactive you'll tend to become. Try it for yourself. Spend an entire morning solely working. No emails. No social media. Then see what happens to your productivity.

* * *

Action step

Using your action guide, optimize your digital environment:

- Turn off phone notifications.
- Check your emails as few times as possible (if possible, limit your email access to once or twice per day).
- Turn off Wi-Fi or stay away from social media or any other sources of online distraction (i.e., install software to remove distractions as and when necessary).
- Unsubscribe from newsletters.

Now let's see what you can do to start building unshakeable confidence to help you act in a way that matches your new model of reality.

2

DEVELOPING UNSHAKEABLE
CONFIDENCE

Believing in something is one of the fundamental steps to achieving anything. You will only take the necessary action to achieve your goals when you truly believe success is possible.

- When you truly believe that you can design a career you enjoy, you will do whatever it takes to get there.
- When you truly believe you deserve to be in a great relationship, you will do whatever is necessary to attract the right person into your life.
- When you truly believe you can retire early, you will create a plan that will help you achieve that goal.

Fortunately, you don't need to develop rock-solid beliefs overnight. Like any other skill, the ability to believe comes with practice. It doesn't matter how low your confidence is right now, you can and will believe in yourself more and more over time as long as you practice consistently.

Next, we will discuss in detail how you can start developing rock-solid confidence in yourself and in your vision. To do so, we'll go over the following:

- Understanding belief.
- Adopting key empowering beliefs.
- Breaking down your goals and developing consistency.
- Conditioning your mind.
- Cultivating self-compassion (or positive self-talk).

A. Understanding belief

Belief cannot be seen or touched, yet it will go a long way to determine whether you will accomplish most of your dreams or none of them, or whether you'll feel good about yourself or inadequate. In this sense, belief is an extremely powerful concept.

Believing means being convinced that you can turn the intangible —an idea or thought—into something tangible—concrete results in the real world. Therefore, learning to believe means trusting yourself enough and understanding the process of creation well enough to turn your goals and dreams into reality.

Few people have developed enough belief to achieve even a fraction of their long-term goals. The good news is that *everyone* can access the power of belief. Once you master the art of belief, everything will change for you and for the people around you. This is because believing not only helps you reach your goals, but it inspires others to do the same. In that sense, believing is like a gift. You can give that gift to yourself or you can offer it to others. By believing in others and giving them a few words of encouragement, you can often help them grow far beyond anything they thought possible. Of course, you can do the same for yourself, too.

Belief is the glue that makes everything possible. It gives you the energy and courage to pursue your goals and to persevere until you achieve the results you long for. When you combine accurate thinking—by redefining your model of reality—with unshakeable belief, the magic happens.

Now one of the most effective ways to develop self-belief is through repetition.

Repetition is how your current beliefs were programmed into your mind. For instance, one of my friends was told by her music teacher that she would never amount to anything and would likely end up as a prostitute, drug addict or alcoholic. She was only ten when this psychological abuse started, and it continued for years. Imagine the impact it had on her emotional development.

You might not have been exposed to such horrific mental harassment, but perhaps your parents told you to find a stable job and ridiculed your dreams. Perhaps they taught you money was evil. Please understand, most of the things you've been told repeatedly have turned into beliefs that are now solidly ingrained in your mind. These beliefs impact your ongoing life decisions and often limit your potential.

I. Understanding the belief building process

I invite you to see the cultivation of self-belief as a process that consists of the following four distinct phases:

1. Not possible. —> 2. Possible. —> 3. Probable. —> 4. Inevitable.

Let's examine each phase briefly.

Phase #1—Not possible

This is when you don't believe that what you want to achieve is possible for you. For instance, it may be when you're convinced that you can't possibly land your ideal job, retire earlier or lose weight. In this phase, you won't even make the attempt because you don't believe you can achieve something. Even if you do try, you'll have little to no conviction and won't be able to obtain any tangible results.

Phase #2—Possible

This is when you ask yourself, "What if?" In this phase, you start believing your goals or dreams may actually be possible. You feel more excited about your goal and become hopeful. Looking at what others have accomplished before, you ask yourself, "Why not me?" You start thinking along the following lines:

- If others can, perhaps I can, too.
- I wonder if I can do X, Y or Z.
- Perhaps if I give it a shot, it could work for me.

Believing something is possible is the first step toward achieving any of your goals. To boost self-belief, you can (among other things):

- Gather case studies of people who have already achieved similar targets,
- Surround yourself with people who have already reached your goals,
- Realize that if others can, you probably can, too,
- Adopt new empowering beliefs that support your goals, and
- Take action in line with your new empowering beliefs.

Phase #3—Probable

This is when you become reasonably confident in your ability to reach your goal. Feeling even more excited, you take more and more action to move toward it. To reach this phase, you'll often need to accumulate small wins consistently over a few weeks or months. You'll also need to surround yourself with positive people who believe in you and support your goals.

Phase #4—Inevitable

This is when you've built enough confidence and have a good enough track record to know—beyond doubt—that you *will* reach your goal. This is the last phase and not an easy one to reach. Although most people don't reach this phase, it doesn't mean you won't. Remember, belief is a skill anybody can develop over time through consistent practice.

Once you become absolutely convinced you are going to achieve the results you seek, self-doubts will disappear and potential roadblocks won't bother you anymore. As a result, you'll be able to focus most of your energy on achieving your goal. With such a high level of certainty, you'll also win over many people around you. You might even feel like the universe is conspiring to *help* you attain your goals.

These are the four phases you will go through as you strengthen your self-belief. As you've discovered, it's not a matter of being born confident or being incredibly smart, it's a matter of following a process and sticking to it long term until your beliefs change radically.

2. The meta-belief that rules all

One specific belief has the power to transform every aspect of your life. This belief will lead you to make the changes needed to design the life you want. Once you start experimenting with it, you'll begin to notice positive changes.

This is the belief that **everything happening to you is the result of your own thinking and everything outside of you is a projection of what's inside you.**

You might be skeptical. However, the point of this belief isn't to be one hundred percent accurate, it is to invite you to look within yourself so that you can make as many positive changes as necessary. This particular belief encourages you to take complete responsibility for your current situation. Furthermore, the more responsibility you assume over your life, the more power you have to change it. As you take action to improve your situation, you'll receive feedback from reality. This feedback will enable you to refine your model of reality.

In other words, this meta-belief eliminates many of your inaccurate assumptions and invites you to discover the truth by yourself. As you change, you'll often find that everything starts changing for you.

So why not behave as though everything happening to you and around you is the result of your thinking? You can then adopt more empowering thoughts that will lead you to take better actions and achieve better results.

3. Using your beliefs to distort reality

Beliefs have the power to "distort" reality. In other words, they can help you influence the reality around you, making it easier for you to achieve concrete results. They do so by:

- Changing your perspective which leads you to take new actions, and
- Changing the way people interact with you.

First, your beliefs have a direct impact on your perspective (i.e., how you see the world). Once you believe something to be true, you'll tend to look for information that validates your belief. Furthermore, you'll tend to act in ways congruent to these same beliefs.

For instance, if you believe you can find your dream job, your brain will start looking for any information that fits that model of reality. You will come across articles featuring people who have switched careers successfully. You will encounter employees who love their jobs, and you will keep seeking more information or evidence you can land your ideal job.

Perhaps we can say that when you change your beliefs, reality changes—or at least *your* reality changes. It's as though you were creating a parallel universe in which another version of you is capable of designing a life in line with your new beliefs.

Second, what you believe changes the way you interact with people and influences your environment. The world isn't something that exists outside of you. You're co-creating it with other people. That is, the actions you take (or fail to take) have a direct impact on your environment. This is why belief is so powerful. When you believe strongly in what you do and act accordingly, you'll start to see that people around you behave differently. People who didn't support you previously will start cheering for you and perhaps they'll even become your biggest fans. They may even start asking for your advice!

As the famous coach, Tony Robbins, said, the most certain person usually wins. This makes belief your superpower. To achieve all your goals and dreams, you must develop the ability to believe, day after day, week after week, month after month. When you truly believe, you'll realize everything will start changing for you.

Unfortunately, many people struggle to believe in themselves. As a result, they become easily influenced by other people. But it doesn't have to be that way. We *can* believe in ourselves. We have the power to develop such a strong vision that nothing and nobody can ever stop us from going after what we want.

B. Adopting key empowering beliefs

What you believe determines the actions you take and therefore, the results you obtain. This is why you must have empowering beliefs that serve you and help you succeed. Now let's review a few empowering beliefs that will make a tremendous difference in your life once you internalize them.

Belief #1—You can improve over the long term

Believing doesn't imply you must be talented and already have all the skills you need. To build confidence, you don't have to be the person you want to be—at least not yet.

True belief means knowing deep down that you can and will improve in the long term. It means developing an inner trust that you *can* figure things out, that you *can* achieve your goals and that you *do* matter. Consequently, it requires you to have faith in yourself and in your ability to grow. It demands you trust yourself and take action to move in the direction you think is right for you.

In her book, *Mindset*, Carol Dweck demonstrated that there are mainly two types of people. People with a *fixed* mindset and people with a *growth* mindset. People with fixed mindsets don't believe they can grow and make major changes in their life. They perceive their abilities as set in stone. On the other hand, people who have growth mindsets believe they can learn and improve. They have the inner belief that they can improve over the long term no matter what.

To sum up, one of the key beliefs required to cultivate confidence is the belief that you can figure things out and that the ability to improve is absolutely inevitable in the long term. This belief permeates everything you do and every thought you have and will help you overcome many of your future challenges.

Belief #2—If someone else can, you can

We all have a fairly similar brain. So if someone else can do something, you can probably do it, too. This is one of the core beliefs I've been relying on for the past few years. Thus, avoid assuming others are smarter or better than you. With enough practice, belief and confidence, if others can do something, you can do it too.

Remember, if you refuse to believe that something is possible for you it will never become your reality. You have to believe something is possible for it to become possible. Of course, this doesn't mean it's going to be easy, but it does mean that with enough practice and with a strong willingness to learn and improve, you'll likely get where you want to be in the future.

Belief #3—If you can do it once, you can do it again

Sometimes to start believing in yourself, all you need to do is something just one time. Imagine if you could do something you thought impossible even just once. How would that change your perspective? What new possibilities would it open up to you?

The point is, you don't need to be making millions with your side hustle or to have tons of clients already lined up. For now, all you need to do is make your first dollar or find your first client. If you can do it once, you know you can make it happen again. No need to doubt yourself, either. That would be wasting your precious energy. So challenge yourself to do the one thing you need to do just once. Then repeat the process. If you can do it once, you can do it again.

Belief #4—Others will give up, therefore, you will succeed

Most people give up way too soon. Don't be one of these people. Stop giving up on your dreams so easily. When things get tough, remember why you started in the first place. Did you tell yourself, "I will give it a shot and give up when everybody else is giving up?" Probably not. Otherwise, why did you even bother starting in the first place? When you can't take it anymore, that's exactly when you need to push through. Keep going. Once you learn to stick to your goals in the long term, you'll be able to achieve almost anything you desire. So stop worrying about the competition. Most people are not your competitors. They will give up way before you do.

Belief #5—Success is inevitable

What if you knew beyond any doubt that you would achieve your goals? We spend an enormous amount of time and energy wondering whether we're going to make it. Inside us, there is a constant battle between the part eager to go after our goals and the part that believes we might fail. To start getting rid of your self-doubts, I invite you to assume your success is inevitable. I encourage you to see yourself as being successful already and to realize that you're resourceful enough to figure things out. Yes, you will probably fail many times along the way, but by pushing through and learning from each setback, you'll eventually reach your goals.

Bear in mind that developing unshakeable confidence isn't about adopting the belief you will not fail. It's about knowing that, no matter how many difficulties you face and no matter how many times you'll fail, you'll eventually figure out a way to get from where you are to where you want to be. Having the inner belief that achieving your goal is just a matter of time is absolutely essential to your long-term success.

In conclusion, assume success is inevitable in the long term. Meanwhile, be willing to fail as many times as necessary in the short term until you obtain the desired results.

To learn how to develop rock-solid confidence and make your success inevitable in greater depth, refer to my book, *Success Is Inevitable*.

When the five beliefs outlined above become part of your identity, your confidence will grow and you will become far more perseverant. This, in turn, will dramatically increase the chance you'll achieve your long-term goals.

* * *

Action step

Print out the page with the five beliefs from your action guide and read them on a regular basis. Think of them often. If you identify other great beliefs you want to adopt, add them to your repertoire.

C. Breaking down your goals and developing consistency

When it comes to developing rock-solid confidence, your ability to set and achieve goals—and do it consistently—is key. After all, if you never do what you promised to do, how rotten are you going to feel about yourself?

Don't worry. There is no need to reach huge goals right off the bat. Repeatedly attaining small goals will help you build the confidence required to achieve the bigger ones.

Setting goals made a major difference in my life. It didn't happen overnight, though. It took me a couple of years to get used to setting and achieving goals. These days, I find it easier to set realistic goals and ones I'll actually achieve.

Five years ago, I wrote that, by April 18th, 2020 (my thirty-fifth birthday) I would have written twenty to twenty-five books and would be making $5,000 per month. As I'm writing this, it's February 2020. I'm working on my twentieth book (this one), and I have exceeded my income target. As a side note, I actually threw away the list years ago (sigh).

My point is, setting attainable goals works. But it's a skill that must be acquired through practice. If you want to develop unshakeable confidence, do what you promise to do. Write down your goals, read them regularly, and most importantly, strive to achieve them one after the other.

To make it easy, break down your goals into smaller, more manageable tasks. For instance, break down your five-year vision into annual goals. Then further break down your annual goals into quarterly, monthly, weekly and daily goals. Any goal, no matter how big it may be, can be broken down into small daily tasks. And in the end, achieving these small tasks every single day will lead to extraordinary and powerful results. For example:

- By reading ten pages a day, you will have read fifteen to twenty books in one year (and 150-200 books in ten years),
- By writing 300 words per day, you'll have written three books like this one over a twelve-month period (and 120 books over a forty-year career), and
- By reaching out to one influencer per day, you'll have contacted 365 influencers over a year.

Small tasks do add up over time. So break down your major goals into smaller tasks. This will prevent you from feeling overwhelmed. Attacking a challenge this way, you'll often be surprised by how much you'll achieve in the long term.

Now let's see how you can break your goals down into smaller, bite-sized chunks.

To learn how to become an unstoppable goal achiever in ninety days or less, check my planner, *The Ultimate Goal Setting Planner*.

How to break down your goals

If your goal seems too daunting or unrealistic, you should probably break it down. You want to break any of them down until you feel reasonably confident you will achieve them. There are two ways to do this: you can reduce the scope of your goals, or you can change the timeline. For instance, reducing the scope would mean going for a weight loss goal of ten pounds instead of twenty. Changing the timeline would mean giving yourself an extra six months to reach your weight loss goal of twenty pounds.

D. Conditioning your mind

We've mentioned before that the way you adopt new beliefs is through repetition. In this section, we'll go over a few things you can do to implement new empowering beliefs and condition your mind for success.

1. Using affirmations.
2. Changing your self-talk.
3. Practicing visualization.

1. Using affirmations

Whether you know it or not, you're practicing affirmations every day and you've been doing it for years. Through your inner dialogue, you continuously affirm to yourself who (you think) you are. By doing so, you reinforce your sense of identity. Perhaps you affirm to yourself that you're not good enough, you don't deserve to be happy, you won't meet your ideal partner or you will never make money doing what you love. You may see yourself as lazy, shy or uninteresting. Now is any of this really true? Well, it doesn't matter because if you *think* it is, this will most likely become your reality (i.e., the way you perceive yourself).

The good news is that you don't need to tell yourself you're an incompetent and unworthy human being. You can choose to see yourself the opposite way. In short, you can decide to replace your current identity (or part of it) with a new one that will support the kind of life you want to create more effectively. And you can start doing so right now.

Affirmations are statements you repeat to yourself to reprogram your mind and create a more empowering story or identity. The same way you've been told the same negative things over and over, you can tell yourself positive and empowering things over and over again. As Muhammad Ali said, *"It's the repetition of affirmations that leads to belief. And once that belief becomes a deep conviction, things begin to happen."*

Now you might wonder, what kind of affirmations should you tell yourself every day? The answer is, it depends on what aspect of your life you want to change and what disempowering beliefs you currently hold. In the next section, we'll see how you can identify your most liming beliefs and replace them with more empowering ones using tailored affirmations.

Identifying your limiting beliefs

Limiting beliefs are those beliefs you've accepted as true—whether consciously or unconsciously—that limit your field of possibilities.

The simplest and most effective way to identify your limiting beliefs is to look at areas of your life you're not satisfied with and ask yourself why. Your answers to these questions are likely to be limiting beliefs. More specifically, you can ask yourself the following questions for each area of your life:

Why am I not where I want to be in this area? What's holding me back?

For example:

- Why am I not where I want to be in my career? What's holding me back?

- Why am I not where I want to be with my finances? What's holding me back?
- Why am I not where I want to be in my relationships? What's holding me back?

For this exercise, I recommend you use your previous goal and identify the limiting beliefs you hold regarding that specific goal. Why haven't you achieved it yet? What's standing in your way?

Once you have identified some of your limiting beliefs, turn them into positive affirmations. Below are some examples of ways you can turn limiting beliefs into positive affirmations:

- Limiting belief: I don't have enough time to work on my side hustle.
- Positive affirmation: I make the time to do whatever I'm committed to.

- Limiting belief: I don't believe I can find a job I enjoy.
- Positive affirmation: I am finding creative ways to enjoy my job. Every day, I'm moving closer to designing my ideal career.

- Limiting belief: I'm not good enough.
- Positive affirmation: I am good enough and I'm moving closer to my goal every day.

Here are a few tips you can use to create your own affirmations:

- **State your affirmation in the present tense.**
- **Avoid using negatives** and state your affirmation in the positive form. For instance, say "I'm courageous" rather than "I'm no longer afraid."
- **Aim to change your physiological state.** Engage your

body and experiment with different vocal tones. This will add power to your affirmation.

- **Use the power of visualization.** See yourself in specific situations that relate to your affirmation, then try to feel as though you already have what you want. Engaging your emotions this way will make your affirmation significantly more powerful (see also the section, *Practicing visualization*).

Once you have your affirmations, spend a few minutes every day repeating them and/or writing them down. Do your best to engage all your emotions. The more emotional your affirmations are, the more effective they will be.

You can repeat your affirmations first thing in the morning or last thing at night. This is when your subconscious is at its most receptive. You can also repeat your affirmations on your way to work, in the shower or anywhere else you want.

* * *

Action step

Using your action guide, create your own affirmations.

2. Changing your self-talk

Another way to reprogram your mind is through positive self-talk. Like most people, you might be overly harsh with yourself, relying on self-criticism rather than words of encouragement. Fortunately, you have the ability to change the way you talk to yourself and adopt much more positive self-talk. As you do so, your overall mood will improve, your motivation will increase, and your overall confidence will grow.

Now what is self-talk? In a nutshell, self-talk is your internal dialogue. The way you talk to yourself shapes your reality and determines how you feel and what you believe is or isn't possible.

The main difference between positive self-talk and affirmations is that while affirmations tend to be simple sentences such as, "I'm worthy of love" or "I love being confident", positive self-talk is more of a conversation with yourself. In this conversation, each sentence aims to change one or more of the limiting beliefs that prevent you from achieving your goals. By addressing each one, you can make positive changes in your life.

If we take money as an example, your limiting beliefs could be:

- Money is not important.
- Money is the root of all evil.
- I wish we could live in a world with no money.
- To make more money I must take it from someone else who needs it.
- I need money to make money.
- I need to know the right people to make money.
- To make money, I must be dishonest.
- I'm not worthy enough to charge more for my products or services.
- I can't be spiritual *and* wealthy.
- If I make money, people around me will resent me.
- If I become wealthy, I'll only attract people interested in my money.
- Money is scarce and there isn't enough for everyone.
- Making money is hard.
- I'm not good with money.

Now here is what your self-talk regarding money could look like.

"The more money I make, the more people I can help. Being wealthy allows me to give more money to charity and invest in projects I truly believe in. For me, money is a just spiritual tool I can use to express my

deepest convictions and do good in the world. I strive to earn it, spend it and invest in ways that fall in line with my core values and aspirations. Because I value myself and my work, I'm happy to be well rewarded financially for the products and services I offer. I also know I can always improve my skills and create more value. This means I can always find ways to make more money. And the more money I make, the more freedom I have to pursue the things that matter to me. With all the technologies and free sources of information available, making money has never been easier than it is today."

Now, this is just an example. It's up to you to talk to yourself in a way that feels natural and resonates with you. Of course, your self-talk will vary based on the limiting beliefs you want to overcome. Alternatively, you'll find self-talk audio tracks on YouTube. Feel free to listen to them as well.

Remember, beliefs are created through repetition as well as through emotions. The more you repeat something to yourself, and the more emotionally charged it is, the stronger that belief will be and the deeper it will sink in. For example, if you associate money with freedom and keep repeating to yourself what a wonderful agent for freedom money is and the deeper you feel it, the stronger that belief will become.

Let's return to your previous goal. Look at everything you believe is holding you back in regards to that goal. Do you have your list? Now let's imagine you're talking to a friend that holds the same beliefs. Try to convince him that the opposite is true.

Now it's your turn to create your own self-talk and start eliminating your restrictive beliefs.

* * *

Action step

Using your action guide, write down a few sentences you can use as positive self-talk to overcome some of the limiting beliefs you hold relating to your goal.

3. Practicing visualization

Your imagination is one of your most valuable assets. It's more powerful than willpower and bypasses logic. When used effectively, it can help you achieve almost anything you desire. Anything you visualize strongly enough and for long enough will tend to become your reality. This is because as you keep visualizing, you will feel compelled to take action to close the gap between what you see in your mind and what you want to manifest in reality. In addition, as you tell your subconscious mind what you want to happen, you'll find yourself spotting new opportunities or meeting new people who can help you on your journey. Therefore, to feed your new model of reality, you must keep visualizing what you want to see happen in the future until you firmly believe it will become your reality.

Remember, we do not perceive reality as it *actually* is, but as we *think* it is. Our version of reality is tainted by our biases, limiting beliefs and life experiences. Now you can choose to hold onto a whole bunch of limiting beliefs, or you can let go of them and use your imagination to develop a new reality in which you're much more powerful, determined and confident.

Below are a few simple steps to get started with visualization.

1) Relax

The more relaxed you are, the more effective visualization will be. As you put yourself in a deep state of relaxation, you'll gain better access to your subconscious. As a result, your subconscious will accept what you visualize more readily without the mental noise and objections you often get from your conscious mind. Also, remember that your mind is at its most receptive first thing in the morning and last thing at night. These are great times to practice visualization.

2) Visualize what you want

Your imagination is limitless. Therefore, there is no situation you cannot create in your mind. Whatever you decide to visualize, try to make it as specific and clear as possible. An effective way to do so is by creating a mental movie. Put yourself inside the move and make it appear as if it were happening right here, right now.

Think about it this way: when you think of past events, do you remember specific memories or just fixed images? You need to create mental movies similar to the memories you would have if what you desire had already happened or was actually happening. For example, if you want to travel the world, don't just list the name of the countries you want to visit, see yourself walking the streets, visiting famous monuments and eating at local restaurants. Be specific. Where are you staying? What are you eating? Who are you with?

Visualizing is not merely daydreaming. The "One day I will" type of thinking seldom, if ever, materializes. This is nothing more than wishful thinking. Conversely with visualization, there is desire and commitment. It doesn't mean you need to be tense or stressed about it, though. Just relax and trust that your desire and commitment will help you reach your goals.

3) Feel as though you're already there

Emotions drive actions. When you feel good, you're more creative, more resourceful and more productive. When you are in a positive frame of mind, you readily take the actions you need to achieve your goals. Therefore, whenever you visualize, engage as many of your emotions as possible. Feel excited about your vision. More specifically, feel as if you are already the person you want to be and you already have the things you want. For instance, if you want to be confident, see yourself being confident in a variety of situations. Create a mental movie and revisit it over and over again. Feel confident while you make a presentation at work. See yourself relaxed as you attend a social event. Imagine people around you being friendly and receptive.

Feelings are important because they allow you to shift your beliefs quickly and profoundly. As your beliefs change, your subconscious will try to align the reality around you with your new reality. As a result, you'll find yourself taking more actions to close the gap between where you are and where you believe you must be.

If you feel any resistance when you visualize, acknowledge it, let it go and refocus on the object of your visualization.

4) Focus on what you want as often as possible

Here again, repetition is key. Spend time every day visualizing the person you want to become. Step into your vision first thing in the morning and see yourself as the person you want to be. Keep visualizing this same thing throughout the day. Then do the same at night before going to bed. Keep feeling as though you're already that person. Assume that the qualities you seek to develop are already inside you just waiting to be uncovered.

The repetition of an emotionalized vision will lead you to take different actions. Over time, these new actions will move you closer to the person you want to become.

These are the four simple steps to effective visualization.

The bottom line is this: you can tap into your imagination 24/7. Therefore, make sure you use it to create your ideal life, not to revisit unhappy memories or worry about your future. What you think about often and for long enough will tend to become your reality—but only if you take action, of course.

* * *

Action step

Spend a few minutes every morning visualizing yourself moving toward your goal and accomplishing it. Additionally, think about your goals throughout your day.

E. Cultivating self-compassion (or positive self-talk)

Developing the unshakeable confidence that you need to achieve your goals isn't simply about being confident all the time. You may fall prey to self-doubt from time to time and that's okay. The power of belief arises when you're able to maintain a high level of belief in yourself and in your vision over long periods. We all know people who are excited about their new goals and are ready to take on the world. They may seem completely determined, working hard on their goals for days, weeks or even months. However, they soon start doubting themselves when results fail to match their expectations. As a result, they give up.

On the other hand, true belief lasts day after day, week after week, month after month, year after year. You must develop the ability to keep believing long term no matter what. Self-compassion plays an important role in this regard. Having enough self-compassion will help you maintain confidence. At the same time, it will prevent you from feeling sad or discouraged. In short, it will act as a safety net to your emotional well-being, allowing you to persevere during challenging times. As such, it is an integral part of the confidence-building process required to achieve any of your long-term goals.

1. Understanding self-compassion

The first step toward becoming more self-compassionate is to understand a few simple truths that will help you replace your model of reality with a more empowering and compassionate one.

Truth #1—You're doing the best you can with what you have

It's easy to beat yourself up when you feel as though you're not living up to your true potential. The truth is, you'll never be able to unlock one hundred percent of your capabilities. The reason is simple: while your potential is almost unlimited, your time isn't.

The first truth I want to share with you is this: you're always doing the best you can with what you have. For instance, let's say you're procrastinating on a project. This isn't a sign you should be more productive nor is it an invitation to beat yourself up. It's simply a sign the current version of you is procrastinating due to fear, lack of clarity or perhaps low energy levels. In that very moment, procrastinating is the best you can do. Of course as you develop, the You 2.0 will become better at dealing with procrastination and other issues.

The point is, you're always doing the best you can with what you have. So is everybody else. Therefore, when you feel the urge to criticize yourself, remember that. Be kind to yourself. It's the best thing to do.

Truth #2—You're exactly where you're supposed to be

This leads us to the second truth: you're exactly where you're supposed to be *right now*. Because if you weren't, you would be somewhere else. So do the best you can where you are and encourage yourself along the way. By doing so, you'll end up in a much better place in the future.

Truth #3—You don't need to be perfect in any way

Do you feel discouraged when you look at all the people who are better, smarter, stronger or happier than you? Realize that there will always be people who are doing better than you in certain areas of life.

The real battle you have isn't with other people, it's with yourself. Others have their own issues you know nothing about. Let them deal with their own problems. Meanwhile, refocus on yourself and on what you can do to improve your situation.

Every human being has flaws. Fortunately, you don't need to be perfect to design a great life; you simply need to acknowledge your strengths and nurture them. You have a few abilities no other human being has. Why not focus on these abilities and see what you can create with them?

The point is, you don't need to be perfect to be successful. You only need to identify your biggest strengths and express them the best you can at your own pace while being kind to yourself.

Truth #4—You're not alone

Whatever challenges you're going through right now, you're not alone. Other people have similar issues or worse. Recognizing the fact that you're not alone is part of the process required to cultivate self-compassion. Whenever you feel lonely or misunderstood, understand that many people are going through similar challenges right now. You are not alone.

Truth #5—You have time

We've already touched upon the importance of thinking long term, but it's worth repeating. You have time to grow. It's okay if things take more time than you hoped, and it's often to be expected. But it's not a reason to lose confidence or give up. Stick to whatever major goals you want to achieve. Give yourself time and remain optimistic no matter what. See failures as invitations to grow. And, most importantly, always be kind to yourself.

2. Practicing self-compassion

Self-criticism is a habit as is self-compassion. You can learn to respect and encourage yourself during challenging times. You can become your best coach and most avid supporter. There is nothing wrong or selfish in doing so. You deserve every bit of it. Below are a couple of things you can do to practice self-compassion:

- Use self-compassion during challenging times.
- Undertake a 7-day challenge.

a. Using self-compassion during challenging times

Self-compassion is one of the most useful tools available to you during difficult times. Whether you failed an exam, were rejected by your date or became sick, remember to be self-compassionate.

Self-compassion is the best antidote against negative emotions. It will prevent you from becoming miserable and will protect you against sadness, self-criticism, shame or guilt. It will help you persevere, turning you into bamboo that never breaks, but always bounces back to its original, upright position.

I started practicing self-compassion a few years ago. Whenever I noticed I was being hard on myself, I would change my self-talk. Instead of telling myself I was stupid, I would tell myself that it's okay to make mistakes, that I would do better next time, that I tried my best or whatever else was relevant to the situation.

Did it make me complacent?

No.

Did I slack off and become a couch potato?

No.

In fact, I've probably never been as productive in my life. My point is, you don't need to be hard on yourself to become a top performer and achieve everything you desire. You don't need to rely on fear, shame or guilt. Neither do you need to belittle yourself, hoping you'll finally goad yourself into doing the things you want to do. Trying to rule by fear shows a lack of self-trust and a lack of understanding in the power of self-love. So stop ruling yourself by fear. Instead, use inspiration and self-compassion as your primary motivators. Develop trust in yourself and start talking to yourself as you would talk to your best friend or your loved one. Then see how quickly things change in your life and for the better.

b. Undertaking a 7-day challenge

Here is a practical exercise you can do. For the next seven days, refrain from criticizing yourself. Every time you talk to yourself in a negative way, stop and replace your criticisms with kind words such as, "you're doing okay", "you'll do better next time" or "you made a mistake, but it's okay".

If you want, you can also put a rubber band around your wrist and snap it each time you notice you're being harsh on yourself. Criticizing yourself is a habit and, as with any other habit, you can break it and replace it with a better one.

Action step

Using your action guide, complete the exercises below:

- Undertake a 7-day self-compassion challenge.
- Whenever you notice you start beating yourself up, change your self-talk. Tell yourself you're doing okay. Encourage yourself. Be kind to yourself.

Ideally, the belief you will achieve your goals should be a 7 or 8 out of 10. If you're new to goal setting, you might want to aim for a 9 out of 10. Remember, in the short term, what matters most is that you build the track record of success. You must turn yourself into a person who actually achieves his or her goals. Over time, this will boost your confidence and help you generate momentum. Consistency matters far more than intensity. Expert goal achievers aren't necessarily the hardest workers, but they are definitely the most consistent.

To sum up, set small goals and then achieve them. Do what you say you will do. This will enhance your self-confidence and build your sense of self-trust and self-worth.

3. Setting daily goals

Achieving goals consistently is a wonderful way to build confidence and generate momentum. But how do you do it? Here is what you can do: set three small daily goals you know you will achieve. To do so, after you wake up every morning, take a piece of paper (or use a notebook or a computer) and write down three tasks you want to complete that day. The tasks should be easy enough so that you're almost guaranteed to finish them. Then complete them one hundred percent. Repeat the process for at least thirty days in a row. Doing this will allow you to build your confidence and boost your self-esteem.

What we're doing here is building a new identity, the identity of someone who set goals and achieves them over and over and who, whenever he or she says something, means it. The more you set and achieve daily goals, the more confident you'll become and the bigger goals or projects you'll be able to tackle.

Here's a word of caution: goal setting isn't an exact science. Occasionally you will fail to achieve some of your goals, especially at the beginning. This is perfectly fine. Be kind to yourself and keep going. Your goal-achieving skills will improve over time.

If you want to learn how to set and achieve exciting goals, refer to my book, *Goal Setting*.

* * *

Action step

Complete the exercises below using your action guide:

- Re-using the goal you've been working with, break it down into yearly, monthly, weekly and daily goals.
- For the next thirty days, set three simple daily tasks and make sure you complete them.

3

EXPAND YOUR FIELD OF POSSIBILITIES

What you can and cannot do is largely determined by your mindset. When you develop a powerful mindset, a whole new world of opportunity opens up to you. Your thinking starts shifting, your confidence grows and what you thought was impossible becomes your new reality.

In this section, we'll discover what you can do to expand your field of opportunity and find yourself in a positive emotional state that will enable you to tackle new challenges. After all, having an accurate model of reality is useless unless you're able to take the action required to achieve your goals.

To help you expand your field of possibilities we'll cover the following topics:

- Generating luck.
- Asking yourself empowering questions.
- Taking consistent action.
- Leveraging the power of gratitude.

Let's get started.

A. Generating luck

I'm not a big believer in luck. I believe it is our responsibility to do whatever it takes to "become lucky". The truth is, in most cases, the more action we take, the more likely we are to generate our own "luck" at some point.

For instance, the way I approached my publishing business was to release book after book consistently until one of my books took off. Having analyzed other successful indie others, I understood I would likely need to have quite a few books out before I could expect any kind of traction. Eventually, this is what happened. One book took off. Then another one. And another one. In a sense, I got "lucky".

In short, the best way to become "lucky" is to take massive and continuous action until something works. Of course, as we've discussed, your actions should be part of an effective overall strategy.

Now does this mean you're guaranteed to achieve the results you want? No. Very few things, if any, are guaranteed in life—except perhaps the fact you must pay taxes and will die one day. But taking action increases your chance of success.

Here are some ways you can manufacture luck:

1. Refusing to believe in luck,
2. Repeatedly thinking about what you want,
3. Broadcasting your desires to the world,
4. Taking consistent action in line with a clearly defined strategy, and
5. Learning as much as you can from the feedback you receive from reality (based on your actions).

Let's look at each of these briefly.

1. Refusing to believe in luck

People who refuse to see luck as the determining factor for their long-term success gain immediate power over their lives. They take one hundred percent responsibility, realizing they can always try new things and refine their model of reality. They understand that for things to change, *they* will have to change. With this mindset, they tend to achieve better results than most people.

Conversely, people who believe they need to be lucky to become successful fail to realize how much power they have to transform their lives. They think the game is rigged and the odds are stacked against them. As a result, all they can hope for is to get lucky. This is why they often play the lottery or gamble, hoping to win big one day.

You must realize there is always something you can do to improve your situation. There are always options. Every passing second offers countless opportunities. Because you can always think better thoughts and take different actions, you can always change your future.

2. Repeatedly thinking about what you want

Another way to "manufacture" luck is to keep thinking about what you want over and over again. By thinking of what you want every day, you tell your subconscious to look for ways to make your goal a reality. As a result, your subconscious will work 24/7 to help you reach your goal. Cool, isn't it?

So keep thinking about what you want. Visualize your future vividly and feel the emotions you will experience once you reach your goal.

3. Broadcasting your desires to the world

To receive help, you must let people know exactly what you're trying to accomplish. Most people would be willing to help you provided they knew how. The more specific you are, the more people will be in the position to give you sound advice or introduce you to someone who will.

4. Taking consistent action in line with a clearly defined strategy

Another way to generate luck is to take more action in the real world. Now the point is not to take random actions or fall for short-term tricks or gimmicks, hoping you'll achieve some success. The idea is to take actions that are aligned with your strategy. The more of these actions you take, the more likely you are to get lucky.

5. Learning as much as you can from the feedback you receive from reality

The more action you take, the more feedback you will receive from reality. By learning from feedback and adjusting your actions accordingly, you will create a better model of reality which will involve higher quality assumptions. Armed with sound assumptions, you'll make better decisions and achieve superior results. In short, we can sum up the process as follows:

More action. —> More feedback. —> Better assumptions. —> Better actions. —> Better results.

Always make sure you are continuously learning from your mistakes. As you do so, you'll achieve much better results in the long term.

* * *

Action step

Using your action guide, complete the corresponding exercises to start generating more luck.

B. Asking yourself empowering questions

This is a great way to guide your thinking and invite smart answers that inspire effective actions. Now let's see what the different types of empowering questions are.

1. "How" questions

I love "how" questions because they invite you to search for solutions. Instead of telling yourself your biggest goals are impossible, it is far more empowering to look at your goals and ask yourself how you can achieve them. As you brainstorm ways to reach your goals, you'll come up with many great ideas and will feel inspired to take action and press forward. Whenever you find yourself thinking "I can't do this", immediately erase that thought and ask yourself, "How can I do this?"

- I can't make a living doing what I love. —> *How can I make a living doing what I love?*
- I can't retire before I'm sixty-five. —> *How can I retire before I'm sixty-five?*
- Now that I have kids, I can't travel as much as I'd like to. —> *How I can I travel with kids?*

Thinking you can't do something is never a good idea. For sure, there are certain things you genuinely can't do, but whenever you find yourself thinking you can't do something, ask yourself the question "How can I?" instead. Then see what answers you come up with.

2. "What if" questions

"What if" questions are great because they leverage the power of your imagination, one of the most powerful tools in your arsenal. They also remove some pressure from your shoulders since you don't need to believe you can do something (yet). More specifically, the questions I have in mind here are "What if I can" questions. Below are some examples:

- What if I can make a living doing what I love?
- What if I can retire at forty-five?
- What if I can travel extensively with my kids?

Remember, we are the only species on earth that can imagine a better future and make it a reality by forming a plan and acting on it consistently. It's our superpower. So what if you could design your ideal life in the coming years? What if you could have (almost) everything you want?

By using "What if" questions you'll open yourself up to new opportunities. And as you keep taking action repeatedly, you'll be able to create a more empowering model of reality that will lead to better results. So keep asking yourself, "What if".

* * *

Action step

Write down the answer to the questions below using your action guide:

- How can I achieve my goal? What can I do to help me reach it?
- What if I could achieve my goal? What if it was possible?

C. Taking consistent action

To develop the beliefs necessary to reach your goals, you must receive feedback from reality. And the best way to do this is by taking consistent action.

I. The benefits of taking action

Taking action comes with several benefits.

First, it allows you to identify what works and what doesn't. There may be things you believe could be effective, but don't actually work. In short, taking action is a great way to test your assumptions.

Second, taking consistent action allows you to shatter your beliefs regarding what is and isn't possible for you. For instance, you might believe you could never give a speech in front of a large audience, write a book or run a marathon. However, as you begin to take action, you may realize it's actually possible. And the more you accumulate small wins, the more your confidence will grow and the more action you'll be able to take.

Third, taking action enables you to refine your model of reality even further. For example, if you take consistent action for months but fail to see positive results, you might start questioning what you're doing. Perhaps you're doing the wrong thing, or not taking enough action. Such questioning will lead you to adjust your actions until you begin to notice tangible results. Remember, we're living in a world ruled by cause and effect. Certain actions are likely to generate the results you're looking for while others aren't. It doesn't matter how much you *say* you want to help people, how good a person you are or how hard you work. What matters are the outcomes. The real questions you must answer are:

- How accurate is my model of reality?
- How effective is my current blueprint?

- Am I truly taking all the necessary actions to reach my goal?

Maybe you believe you should be a motivational speaker because you care so much about others. Or maybe you think you deserve to be a professional singer because you've been singing every day for years. However, the only thing that matters in the end is how accurate your model of reality is, how closely it aligns with the world out there, and how well you're acting on it.

The bottom line is, for whatever goal you pursue, you need to run an audit and be radically honest with yourself. Many people delude themselves and become bitter when they fail to reach their goals. Don't become one of those people. Instead, do whatever it takes to achieve your goals or go do something else which would be fine, too.

* * *

Action step

Using your action guide, answer the following questions:

- How well is my current approach working for me?
- Am I really taking enough action to reach my goal?
- What would taking massive action mean to me?

2. Doubling down on what works

As you repeatedly take action and test your assumptions, you'll discover that a couple of things you do work very well. Perhaps your audience loves one of your products. Perhaps one of your services is generating more money than all the others combined. If so, start focusing more of your time and resources on activities that already deliver results.

Now you might find it counterintuitive to neglect products or services you spent so much time creating. You might think you should work on increasing the sales of your worst-selling products or services. However, this is often a mistake. Boosting the sales of an already popular product is usually far easier than trying to get an unpopular one to sell. In the former case, the ball is already rolling and you just need to give it an extra push.

To give you an example, I chose to optimize the sales of my best-selling book while "giving up" on my non-performing books. To increase sales, I tested different pricing, optimized the book description, and ran tons of ads. I also started translating the books into French, German and Spanish with the assumption it might sell well in these countries, too. Finally, I created a whole series around the book encouraging new readers to go back and read the first book in the series. By doing so, I was able to increase sales significantly.

The point is, keep testing your assumptions until you find something that works. When you do, focus most of your effort on scaling that thing up. Yes, it might feel counterintuitive. Yes, you might feel as though you're missing out on other opportunities. But as we've seen before, you have to miss out on many things to be successful. That's just to be expected.

Action step

Using your action guide, answer the following questions:

- What if anything is bringing me the best results?
- What could I do to double down on that success?

D. Leveraging the power of gratitude

I believe gratitude is one of the most powerful forces on earth. As you develop more gratitude, you'll find that all sorts of things will start changing in your life. Cultivating gratitude doesn't just allow you to develop a deeper sense of appreciation, it also changes how you see the world and the action you take as a result of that transformation.

When you're able to experience gratitude for everything you have in life, you feel more inspired and have more energy to put toward the achievement of your goals and dreams. You feel a renewed sense of possibility, and new opportunities start appearing. As such, developing gratitude is a wonderful way to supercharge your model of reality.

When you're happy with the things you already have, the universe often gives you more—or so it seems. In short, the more you focus on what you have, the more likely you are to get what you want.

So what are you grateful for in your life?

1. Understanding gratitude

Before we see how to cultivate gratitude, let's consider a few limiting beliefs that may prevent you from experiencing more of it.

Belief #1—There is a limited supply of ...

Have you ever thought you will never be able to make your money back, find a partner as good as your previous one or be happy again?

This type of thinking is based on the belief there is a limited supply of things, people or experiences available to you. But is this true?

Sure, there may be important events you might not want to miss, such as weddings and birthdays. However, there is no shortage of amazing events or opportunities available to you in the future. You can always create wonderful memories, can't you? For instance, missing out on an opportunity to make money isn't an issue. There will be more opportunities in the future. And the better you train yourself to spot those opportunities, the more you'll find. There are also many people out there who could be suitable partners for you. Breaking up with someone you love by no means indicates you'll never meet another suitable partner in the future.

The bottom line is, stop being afraid of missing out. Seize opportunities whenever you can but, remember there is and will always be an abundance of opportunities out there.

Belief #2—I'm entitled to a great life

Nowadays, many people take everything they have for granted. However, the truth is, you aren't entitled to anything. The universe doesn't owe you a single thing. Everything you have is temporary and borrowed. Eventually it will have to be returned.

Having an attitude of gratitude requires you to realize how blessed you are to have access to all the comforts modern life has to offer. Many of the benefits you take for granted were things previous generations fought for, whether it be paid holidays, healthcare or the right to vote.

Everything you have is a gift. Make sure you appreciate it fully. Spending time focusing on all the things you already have will help you feel more grateful and develop a deeper sense of abundance.

Belief #3—I need more ...

While there is nothing wrong with wanting more, it can turn into a never-ending pursuit that leaves you deeply unsatisfied—unless you develop gratitude. You don't necessarily need more in life. Often, what you need is to appreciate more of what you already have. It is:

- Appreciating your money and what it pays for instead of being obsessed with becoming more wealthy,
- Nurturing your current relationships with your family and friends rather than trying to make more friends, and
- Counting your blessings instead of counting your misfortunes.

So if you find yourself thinking "I need more *fill in the blank*", question this assumption. Do you really need more, or do you need to appreciate what you have more?

2. Practicing gratitude

Gratitude is a skill and as with any other skill it requires consistent practice. In his book, *Unlock Gratitude*, my friend, Mike Pettigrew, talks about his "Crazy Gratitude Experiment". He was going through a difficult period in his life. After having trusted the wrong person and moving into the wrong type of business, he found himself penniless, unable to feed his wife and his new baby boy. It was one of the most frightening experiences of his entire life as he recalls. That's when he decided to try his crazy gratitude experiment inspired by a book he read.

"Amazingly, by doing my crazy gratitude experiment every thirty minutes of the day, things started to change within only a few days. This was wonderful to see and a great encouragement. Everything started to change as soon as I created this experiment and really tested it. After all, I'd almost nothing else to lose since we were already broke. So, I invented this experiment and tested it and the results were truly incredible."

Of course, he still had to work hard to change his financial situation. But practicing gratitude allowed him to start thinking more positively, and this began to impact his feelings and actions.

To start experiencing the benefits of gratitude, I recommend you spend a few minutes to practice gratitude every day. By doing so over time, you will find it easier to feel grateful even when things don't go the way you want.

Below are a few exercises you can choose from.

a. Writing down things you're grateful for. Take a pen and a sheet of paper, or even better, a dedicated notebook, and write down at least three things for which you are hugely grateful. This will help you focus on the positive side of things.

b. Thanking people who crossed your path. Close your eyes and think of people you've met. As you picture them one after the other, thank them while acknowledging at least one good thing they did for you. If you happen to picture people you don't like, thank them anyway and still look for one good thing they did for you. It could be making you stronger or teaching you a specific lesson. Don't try to control your thoughts; simply let the faces of people you know come to your mind. Release any resentment you feel or have felt for them.

c. Focusing on one object and appreciating its existence.

- Select one item in your room and think of the amount of work and the number of people involved in the process of creating it and delivering it to you. For instance, if you select a chair, think of all the work necessary to create it. Someone had to design it, others had to source the raw materials, and others had to assemble it. Truck drivers had to deliver it to the store. The store employees had to display it and promote it. You or someone else had to collect it. The car you drive also had to be built by other people, and so on.
- Think of how you benefit from the chair. Remember a time you were so tired you couldn't wait to sit. Didn't it feel great when you could finally collapse into it? Thanks to the chair you can not only sit, but you can also use your

computer, write, read, drink coffee or have a pleasant conversation with your friends.

d. Listening to gratitude songs/guided meditation. Listen to gratitude meditation. To find the right song or meditation for you, search "gratitude meditation" on YouTube.

* * *

Action step

Practice one of the exercises below for at least fourteen days:

- Write down things you're grateful for.
- Thank people who crossed your path.
- Focus on one object and appreciate its existence.
- Listen to gratitude songs/guided meditation.

CONCLUSION

I would like to congratulate you on reading this book until the end. I hope reading it has helped you develop a better understanding of the way reality works. I also hope that you've started working on specific ways to develop a more accurate vision of reality. Remember, the more accurate your vision of reality is, the better results you'll tend to achieve when acting on your developed long-term strategy—whether it is related to your career, relationships, finances or health.

Don't deceive yourself. Don't say you want to achieve all these wonderful things while acting in a way that is completely incongruent in your daily life. Take massive, concerted and positive action. Challenge yourself. Try again and again and listen to the feedback that reality gives you. This is how you'll be able to refine your model of reality little by little.

Then work on empowering your model of reality. Create an empowering environment that supports your dreams. Hang out with positive people who will challenge you to become better and aim higher. Develop rock-solid confidence that will impact your own actions and the way people around you behave. In the long term, what you truly believe in will tend to become your reality. So never stop believing and keep doing the work every day.

The person who has the most accurate model of reality and acts accordingly will win. Be that person and wonderful things will happen to you in the near future.

I wish you all the best in all your endeavors.

Warm regards,

Thibaut

Master Your Life With The Mastery Series

This book is the fifth book in the **Mastery Series.** You can check out the the series at the following URL:

mybook.to/Master_Emotions

To read a preview of *Master Your Emotions,* turn the page.

MASTER YOUR EMOTIONS (PREVIEW)

The mind in its own place, and in itself can make a heaven of Hell, a hell of Heaven.

— JOHN MILTON, POET.

We all experience a wild range of emotions throughout our lives. I had to admit, while writing this book, I experienced highs and lows myself. At first, I was filled with excitement and thrilled at the idea of providing people with a guide to help them understand their emotions. I imagined how readers' lives would improve as they learned to control their emotions. My motivation was high and I couldn't help but imagine how great the book would be.

Or so I thought.

After the initial excitement, the time came to sit down to write the actual book, and that's when the excitement wore off pretty quickly. Ideas that looked great in my mind suddenly felt dull. My writing seemed boring, and I felt as though I had nothing substantive or valuable to contribute.

Sitting at my desk and writing became more challenging each day. I started losing confidence. Who was I to write a book about emotions if I couldn't even master my own emotions? How ironic! I considered giving up. There are already plenty of books on the topic, so why add one more?

At the same time, I realized this book was a perfect opportunity to work on my own emotional issues. And who doesn't suffer from negative emotions from time to time? We all have highs and lows, don't we? The key is what we *do* with our lows. Are we using our emotions to grow? Are we learning something from them? Or are we beating ourselves up over them?

So, let's talk about *your* emotions now. Let me start by asking you this:

How do you feel right now?

Knowing how you feel is the first step toward taking control of your emotions. You may have spent so much time internalizing you've lost touch with your emotions. Perhaps you answered as follows: "I feel this book could be useful," or "I really feel I could learn something from this book."

However, none of these answers reflect how you feel. You don't 'feel like this,' or 'feel like that,' you simply 'feel.' You don't 'feel like' this book could be useful, you 'think' this book could be useful, and that generates an emotion which makes you 'feel' excited about reading it. Feelings manifest as physical sensations in your body, not as an idea in your mind. Perhaps, the reason the word 'feel' is so often overused or misused is because we don't want to talk about our emotions.

So, how do you feel now?

Why is it important to talk about emotions?

How you feel determines the quality of your life. Your emotions can make your life miserable or truly magical. That's why they are among the most important things to focus on. Your emotions color all your experiences. When you feel good, everything seems, feels, or tastes better. You also think better thoughts. Your energy levels are higher and possibilities seem limitless. Conversely, when you feel depressed, everything seems dull. You have little energy and you become unmotivated. You feel stuck in a place (mentally and physically) you don't want to be, and the future looks gloomy.

Your emotions can also act as a powerful guide. They can tell you something is wrong and allow you to make changes in your life. As such, they may be among the most powerful personal growth tools you have.

Sadly, neither your teachers nor your parents taught you how emotions work or how to control them. I find it ironic that just about anything comes with a how-to manual, while your mind doesn't. You've never received an instruction manual to teach you how your mind works and how to use it to better manage your emotions, have you? I haven't. In fact, until now, I doubt one even existed.

What you'll learn in this book

This book is the how-to manual your parents should have given you at birth. It's the instruction manual you should have received at school. In it, I'll share everything you need to know about emotions so you can overcome your fears and limitations and become the type of person you really want to be.

You'll learn what emotions are, how they are formed, and how you can use them for your personal growth. You'll also learn how to deal with negative emotions and condition your mind to create more positive emotions.

It is my sincere hope and expectation that, by the end of this book, you will have a clear understanding of what emotions are and will have all the tools you need to start taking control of them.

More specifically, this book will help you:

- Understand what emotions are and how they impact your life
- Identify negative emotions that control your life and learn to overcome them
- Change your story to take better control over your life and create a more compelling future, and
- Reprogram your mind to experience more positive emotions.

Here is a more detailed summary of what you'll learn in this book:

In **Part I**, we'll discuss what emotions are. You'll learn why you are wired to focus on negativity and what you can do to counter this effect. You'll also discover how your beliefs impinge upon your emotions. Finally, you'll learn how negative emotions work and why they are so tricky.

In **Part II**, we'll go over the things that directly impact your emotions. You'll understand the roles your body, your thoughts, your words, or your sleep, play in your life and how you can use them to change your emotions.

In **Part III**, you'll learn how emotions are formed. You'll also learn how to condition your mind to experience more positive emotions.

And finally, in **Part IV**, we'll discuss how to use your emotions as a tool for personal growth. You'll learn why you experience emotions such as fear or depression and how they work. You'll then discover how to use them to grow.

I. What emotions are

Have you ever wondered what emotions are and what purpose they serve?

In this section, we'll discuss how your survival mechanism affects your emotions. Then we'll explain what the 'ego' is and how it impacts your emotions. Finally, we'll discover the mechanism behind emotions and learn why negative emotions can be so hard to deal with.

1. How your survival mechanism affects your emotions

Why people have a bias towards negativity

Your brain is designed for survival, which explains why you're able to read this book at this very moment. When you think about it, the probability of you being born was extremely low. For this miracle to happen, all the generations before you had to survive long enough to procreate. In their quest for survival and procreation, they must have faced death hundreds or perhaps thousands of times.

Fortunately, unlike your ancestors, you're (probably) not facing death every day. In fact, in many parts of the world, life has never been safer. Yet, your survival mechanism hasn't changed much. Your brain still scans your environment looking for potential threats.

In many ways, some parts of your brain have become obsolete. While you may not be seconds away from being eaten by a predator, your brain still gives significantly more weight to negative events than to positive ones.

Fear of rejection is one example of a bias toward negativity. In the past, being rejected from your tribe would reduce your chances of survival significantly. Therefore, you learned to look for any sign of rejection, and this became hardwired in your brain.

Nowadays, being rejected often carries little or no consequence to your long-term survival. You could be hated by the entire world and still have a job, a roof and plenty of food on the table, yet, your brain is still programmed to perceive rejection as a threat to your survival.

This is why rejection can be so painful. While you know most rejections are no big deal, you nevertheless feel the emotional pain. If you listen to your mind, you may even create a whole drama around it. You may believe you aren't worthy of love and dwell on a rejection for days or weeks. Worse still, you may become depressed as a result of this rejection.

In fact, one single criticism can often outweigh hundreds of positive ones. That's why, an author with fifty 5-star reviews, is likely to feel terrible when they receive a single 1-star review. While the author understands the 1-star review isn't a threat to her survival, her authorial brain doesn't. It likely interprets the negative review as a threat to her ego which triggers an emotional reaction.

The fear of rejection can also lead you to over-dramatize events. If your boss criticized you at work, your brain may see the event as a threat and you now think, "What if I'm fired? What if I can't find a job quickly enough and my wife leaves me? What about my kids? What if I can't see them again?"

While you are fortunate to have such an effective survival mechanism, it is also your responsibility to separate real threats from imaginary ones. If you don't, you'll experience unnecessary pain and worry that will negatively impact the quality of your life. To overcome this bias towards negativity, you must reprogram your mind. One of a human being's greatest powers is our ability to use our thoughts to shape our reality and interpret events in a more empowering way. This book will teach you how to do this.

Why your brain's job isn't to make you happy

Your brain's primary job is not to make you happy, but to ensure your survival. Thus, if you want to be happy, you must take control of your emotions rather than hoping you'll be happy because it's your natural state. In the following section, we'll discuss what happiness is and how it works.

How dopamine can mess with your happiness

Dopamine is a neurotransmitter which, among other functions, plays a major role in rewarding certain behaviors. When dopamine is released into specific areas of your brain—the pleasure centers—you get a high. This is what happens during exercise, when you gamble, have sex, or eat great food.

One of the roles of dopamine is to ensure you look for food so you don't die of starvation, and you search for a mate so you can reproduce. Without dopamine, our species would likely be extinct by now. It's a pretty good thing, right?

Well, yes and no. In today's world, this reward system is, in many cases, obsolete. While in the past, dopamine was linked to our survival instinct, The release of dopamine can now be generated artificially. A great example of this effect is social media, which uses psychology to suck as much time as possible out of your life. Have you noticed all these notifications that pop up constantly? They're used to trigger a release of dopamine so you stay connected, and the longer you stay connected, the more money the services make. Watching pornography or gambling also leads to a release of dopamine which can make these activities highly addictive.

Fortunately, we don't need to act each time our brain releases dopamine. For instance, we don't need to constantly check our Facebook newsfeeds just because it gives us a pleasurable shot of dopamine.

Today's society is selling a version of happiness that can make us *un*happy. We've become addicted to dopamine largely because of marketers who have found effective ways to exploit our brains. We receive multiple shots of dopamine throughout the day and we love it. But is that the same thing as happiness?

Worse than that, dopamine can create real addictions with severe consequences on our health. Research conducted at Tulane University showed that, when given permission to self-stimulate their pleasure center, participants did it an average of forty times per minute. They chose the stimulation of their pleasure center over food, even refusing to eat when hungry!

Korean, Lee Seung Seop is an extreme case of this syndrome. In 2005, Mr Seop died after playing a video game for fifty-eight hours straight with very little food or water, and no sleep. The subsequent investigation concluded the cause of death was heart failure induced by exhaustion and dehydration. He was only twenty-eight years old.

To take control of your emotions, it is essential you understand the role dopamine plays and how it affects your happiness. Are you addicted to your phone? Are you glued to your TV? Or maybe you spend too much time playing video games. Most of us are addicted to something. For some people it's obvious, but for others, it's more subtle. For instance, you could be addicted to thinking. To better control your emotions, it is important to shed the light on your addictions as they can rob you of your happiness.

The 'one day I will' myth

Do you believe that one day you will achieve your dream and finally be happy? This is unlikely to happen. You may (and I hope you will) achieve your dream, but you won't live 'happily ever after.' This is just another trick your mind plays on you.

Your mind quickly acclimates to new situations, which is probably the result of evolution and our need to adapt continually in order to survive and reproduce. This is also probably why the new car or house you want will only make you happy for a while. Once the initial excitement wears off, you'll move on to crave the next exciting thing. This phenomenon is known as 'hedonic adaptation.'

How hedonic adaptation works

Let me share an interesting study that will likely change the way you see happiness. This study, which was conducted on lottery winners and paraplegics, was extremely eye-opening for me. Conducted in 1978, the investigation evaluated how winning the lottery or becoming a paraplegic influence happiness:

The study found that one year after the event, both groups were just as happy as they were beforehand. Yes, just as happy (or unhappy). You can find more about it by watching Dan Gilbert's Ted Talk, The Surprising Science of Happiness.

Perhaps you believe that you'll be happy once you've 'made it.' But, as the above study on happiness shows, this is simply not true. No matter what happens to you, you'll revert back to your predetermined level of happiness once you've adapted to the new event. This is how your mind works.

Does that mean you can't be happier than you are right now? No. What it means is that, in the long run, external events have very little impact upon your level of happiness.

In fact, according to Sonja Lyubomirsky, author of *The How of Happiness*, fifty percent of our happiness is determined by genetics, forty percent by internal factors, and only ten percent by external factors. These external factors include such things as whether we're single or married, rich or poor, and similar social influences.

This suggests, only ten percent of your happiness is linked to external factors, which is probably way less than you thought. The bottom line is this: Your attitude towards life influences your happiness, not what happens to you.

By now, you understand how your survival mechanism impacts negatively your emotions and prevent you from experiencing more joy and happiness in your life. In the next segment/section we'll learn about the ego.

To read more visit my author page at:

amazon.com/author/thibautmeurisse

OTHER BOOKS BY THE AUTHORS:

Crush Your Limits: Break Free from Limitations and Achieve Your True Potential (Free Workbook Included)

Goal Setting: The Ultimate Guide to Achieving Life-Changing Goals (Free Workbook Included)

Habits That Stick: The Ultimate Guide to Building Habits That Stick Once and For All (Free Workbook Included)

Master Your Destiny: A Practical Guide to Rewrite Your Story and Become the Person You Want to Be

Master Your Emotions: A Practical Guide to Overcome Negativity and Better Manage Your Feelings (Free Workbook Included)

Master Your Focus: A Practical Guide to Stop Chasing the Next Thing and Focus on What Matters Until It's Done

Master Your Motivation: A Practical Guide to Unstick Yourself, Build Momentum and Sustain Long-Term Motivation

Productivity Beast: An Unconventional Guide to Getting Things Done (Free Workbook Included)

The Greatness Manifesto: Overcome Your Fear and Go After What You Really Want

The One Goal: Master the Art of Goal Setting, Win Your Inner Battles, and Achieve Exceptional Results (Free Workbook Included)

The Passion Manifesto: Escape the Rat Race, Uncover Your Passion and Design a Career and Life You Love (Free Workbook Included)

The Thriving Introvert: Embrace the Gift of Introversion and Live the Life You Were Meant to Live (Free Workbook Included)

The Ultimate Goal Setting Planner: Become an Unstoppable Goal Achiever in 90 Days or Less

Upgrade Yourself: Simple Strategies to Transform Your Mindset, Improve Your Habits and Change Your Life

Wake Up Call: How To Take Control Of Your Morning And Transform Your Life (Free Workbook Included)

ABOUT THE AUTHOR

Thibaut Meurisse is a author, coach, and founder of whatispersonaldevelopment.org.

He has been featured on major personal development websites such as Lifehack, TinyBuddha, MotivationGrid, PickTheBrain, DumbLittleMan or FinerMinds.

Obsessed with self-improvement and fascinated by the power of the brain, his personal mission is to help people realize their full potential and reach higher levels of fulfillment and consciousness.

You can connect with him on his Facebook page

https://www.facebook.com/whatispersonaldevelopment.org

Learn more about Thibaut at

amazon.com/author/thibautmeurisse

ACTION GUIDE

Part I. Letting go of inaccurate thinking

1. The cost of inaccurate thinking

A. Inaccurate thinking creates unnecessary suffering in your life

Write down two or three examples of inaccurate assumptions you may be making right now or have made in the past.

B. Inaccurate thinking leads you to waste time

Look at everything you did this week. Were they all absolutely essential? Were any of these tasks unnecessary?

Write down your answer below:

C. Inaccurate thinking leads you to feel bad about yourself

Write down three situations when you had unrealistic expectations and felt disappointed or frustrated when you failed to achieve your goals or reach your targets.

Situation #1:

Situation #2:

Situation #3:

Then write down your answer to the following questions:

What is one current goal for which you may have unrealistic expectations? How could you adjust your expectations to make them more realistic?

D. Inaccurate thinking leads you to feel overwhelmed

Fill in the table below:

- In the first column, write down all the information you consumed in the past seven days, (e.g. books, articles or emails you read, websites you visited, videos you watched etc.).
- In the second column, write down "U" for useful information or "N" for noise.
- In the third column, write down the concrete actions you will take to deal with information you've identified as noise.

Information consumed in the past 7 days	Useful information (U) or noise (N)	Actions I will take

2. Why your current thinking is inaccurate

A. Poor assumptions distort your thinking

Write down three disempowering assumptions you may be making in your life right now.

Assumption #1:

Assumption #2:

Assumption #3:

Write down one limiting assumption you may have adopted from each of the sources below:

Your parents/family:

Your teachers:

Your friends/peers:

The media:

Your experiences:

Your interpretation:

B. Five common biases that distort your thinking

Write down how each bias plays out in your life. Aim to give at least one specific example for each bias below.

One example of self-serving bias:

One example sunk cost fallacy:

One example of planning fallacy:

One example o survivorship bias:

One example of Dunning-Kruger Effect:

C. How your ego affects your thinking

Write down one specific example from your personal life for each ego activity below:

One example of living in denial:

What I could do about it:

One example of refusing to ask for help:

What I could do about it:

One example of avoiding failures:

What I could do about it:

One example of blaming other people or external circumstances:

What I could do about it:

D. How your emotions distort your thinking

Complete the exercise below:

- Remember a time when everything felt hopeless or gloom and you didn't believe you could be happy again. Then realize your negative emotions eventually faded away.
- Think of three current challenges in your life one after the other. How does each one make you feel? Now, visualize three things you're grateful for or excited about. Feel better?
- Think of one poor decision you made as a result of negative emotions (anger, hopelessness, frustration etc.) or positive emotions (euphoria).
- For one full minute give yourself some words of encouragement. Remind yourself that you're doing okay, that you have good intentions and that you're proud of all the things you've accomplished. How does it make you feel?

3) Three common negative thought patterns to avoid

Thought pattern #1—Generalization

Whenever you find yourself generalizing, reframe the sentence to reflect reality more accurately. See examples below:

I'm always late

—> I may be late more often than I'd like to be, but I'm also on time on many occasions

I'm always the one people make fun of

—> People might make fun of me occasionally, but I'm certainly not the only one. And it doesn't happen all the time.

I never get things right

—> I get things wrong on some occasions, but I get things right many times, too.

Thought pattern #2—All or nothing thinking

Look at each area of your life and see how you may be falling for the all or nothing thinking. Try to come up with specific examples:

Career:

Finance:

Health:

Personal growth:

Relationships:

Spirituality:

Thought pattern #3—Dramatization

Remember one time you worried about something that never happened. Write it down below.

One thing I worried about but that never happened:

Part II. Aligning yourself with reality

1. Accepting reality as it is

Should vs. could

Complete the following exercises:

Write down at least three "should" statements you often use.

Should statement #1:

_____

Should statement #2:

_____

Should statement #3:

_____

Replace "should" by "could" for each statement.

Could statement #1:

_____

Could statement #2:

_____

Could statement #3:

_____

See how it makes you feel and how it changes your thought process.

2. Uncovering your assumptions

A. Identifying your assumptions

Select one important goal and make a list of all the assumptions you may be making about it. We'll keep using this goal for future exercises.

Your goal:

Your assumptions:

-

-

-

-

-

-

-

-

-

-

-

-

-

-

To help you identify your assumptions, please refer to the questions below:

- What are your assumptions regarding the best ways to achieve this goal? What strategies do you assume will work and why?
- Do you think it will be easy or hard and why?
- How long do you think it will take you to reach this goal and why?

B. Testing your assumptions

- Look at your list of assumptions you just wrote down.
- Next to each assumption, write down the accuracy score you would give it on a scale from 1 to 10, (one being completely inaccurate and 10 being one hundred percent accurate).

3. Refining your model of reality

A. Revising your assumptions

What do you know for sure regarding your goal? Write down below assumptions you believe to be correct regarding your goal.

How can you be so certain? Write down the reasons you think you're right.

B. Sharpening your thinking by asking yourself questions

Spend some time answering the questions below to sharpen your thinking.

1) Do I believe I will achieve my goal?

2) Do I have a track record of achieving similar goals?

3) What makes me think I will achieve this goal? What concrete evidence or tangible results are there to support this claim?

4) Do the people around me believe I will achieve my goal?

5) Do I have the energy and/or time required to achieve this goal within the set timeframe?

6) How many people have achieved this goal before? How many people try to achieve it now?

7) Who has achieved that goal before?

8) Why is this goal important to me?

9) If I keep doing what I'm doing every day will I achieve my goals? If not, what exactly needs to change?

10) What are the best approaches/strategies I can follow?

11) What does my intuition tell me to do?

C. Interviewing experienced people

Complete at least one of the exercises below, (and preferably both).

- Ask each question to the relevant person/people
- Watch interviews/read biographies and try answering the question below based on the information you gathered.

1) How does this work?

2) What are the biggest assumptions you make? And how do you know these are accurate or effective?

3) What do I need to understand that I may not understand yet?

4) If you were in my shoes what would you do?

5) If you were to start all over again, what would you do to get results faster?

6) If you had to choose only one activity to focus on, which one would give you the best results?

D. Doing your own research

1) How to find high-quality information

What is the highest quality of information out there and where can you find it? Write down your answer below:

2) How to find the right information for *you*

a. Making sure you have a clearly defined goal

Answer the questions below:

What exactly is my goal? What do I hope to create by using this information?

If I could obtain the perfect information that would guarantee I achieve my goal, what would it look like? How would it be structured?

b. Understanding how the information applies to *you*

Does the recommended blueprint, program or advice apply in my specific case?

Do I have the desire to take action on that information? If not, why not? What changes do I need to make?

c. Ensuring the information is up to date

To ensure the information is up to date, you can ask yourself some of the questions below:

Is this information still relevant today?

How can I make sure it actually is?

If I'm unable to answer the two questions above, do I know someone who does have the answer?

E. Being curious

Remain curious by engaging in the following activities:

- Stay up to date by checking out new publications on a regular basis.
- Identify the experts in your industry and follow them.
- Challenge your assumptions regularly and revise your strategy as necessary.
- See how you can apply ideas or strategies in areas that are unrelated to your goal.
- Look for trends and practice predicting what could happen in the coming years.

F. Listening to your emotions

Answer the following questions:

How motivated do you feel about your goal?

What could you do to boost your motivation? Could you reframe your goal, find out other reasons to incentivize you, or change it altogether?

4. Avoiding common misconceptions and delusional thinking

On a scale from 1 to 10, (1 being irrelevant and 10 being spot on), rate how each of these four misconceptions applies to your specific situation.

Misconception #1—I deserve to be successful

0   10

Misconception #2—I do great work, therefore, I should be successful

0   10

Misconception #3—I'm just one breakthrough away ...

0   10

Misconception #4—I'm already good enough and don't need to improve

0   10

5. How to create an effective process

Write down all the things you could do to achieve your goal. Don't censure or limit yourself. Just write everything that comes to mind. Try to produce at least ten to twenty actions.

Things you could do to achieve your goal:

-

-

-

-

-

-

-

-

-

-

-

-

-

-

-

-

-

A. Narrowing your options

Complete the following exercises:

- Review the ideas you came up with in the previous exercise.
- Come up with at least three possible strategies by combining some of your ideas.
- For each strategy, take a moment to think of all the things this strategy suggests you should *not* be doing.

Strategy #1:

Strategy #2:

Strategy #3:

B. Putting in place an effective process

Complete the exercise below:

Review the strategies you've already identified and select the one you believe to be the best.

Write down the process you think you need to implement to make that strategy work, (e.g. what you need to do every day/regularly to maximize your chances for success).

C. Cultivating long-term thinking

Complete the sentence below with as many answers as you can think of:

If I was better at thinking long term I would:

-

-

-

-

-

-

-

-

5) How to transition from short-term to long-term thinking

a. Creating a long-term vision

Think of a major goal. Then answer the following questions:

What's the ultimate vision behind your goal?

How can you make that goal even more specific?

Why is that goal so important to you?

What financial, physical, mental and/or emotional benefits will you gain from reaching it?

b. Thinking of your long-term goals often

- create a vision board and put it somewhere you'll see it often
- write down your long-term goal on a piece of paper and put it on your desk or somewhere you'll be able to see it daily, and/or
- read your long-term goal every day/week.

c. Dedicating time to focus on the big picture

Carve out time every week to focus on the big picture. To help you do so, go through the list of questions below:

- What am I satisfied with?
- What do I want or need to improve?
- What can I do differently to speed up my progress?
- If I were to start the week all over again, what could I do differently?
- If I keep doing what I've done this week will I achieve my long-term goal? If not, what changes do I need to make?

- Is my current strategy the best one possible? If not, how can I refine it to make it even better?
- What are the very few things that generate most of my results? Can I focus more on these things?
- What are all the things that haven't proven to be effective so far? Can I get rid of some of them?
- If I only work on one thing next week/month, this year, what would be best in terms of overall progress?

d. Learning to love the process

Complete the sentence below.

For me, focusing more on the process would mean:

e. Letting go of the fear of missing out

Complete the exercises below:

Write down the area(s) of your life in which you experience fear of missing out.

-

-

-

-

Select one specific area or goal and write down all the opportunities that actually exist out there. What are all your options? What are all the things you could do?

Your area/goal:

All the options out there/tings you could do:

-

-

-

-

-

-

-

-

-

Take a moment to appreciate all the opportunities available to you.

f. Reminding yourself to be patient

Regularly remind yourself that you have time. To do this, you can:

Create your own mantras such as "life is a marathon, not a sprint", or simply "I have time" or "be patient". Then think of them often, write them down and/or display them on your desk or on your wall.

Watch some of Gary Vaynerchuk's videos on the importance of being patient. Search the following on Youtube

- Gary Vee People Have Forgotten the Art of Patience
- Gary Vee Overnight Success

Visualize everything you've already done in the past few months/years and remind yourself of how much more time you have available.

7-step method to approach any new task

To make sure you're as productive as possible, I encourage you to follow the 7-step process outlined below, before you start any significant task:

Step 1. Prioritizing your task

Before you start working on a task, ask yourself:

- If I could do only one thing today, which task would have the most impact?
- Is this task moving me closer to my main goal?
- Do I really need to do it right now, or can I do it later?

Train yourself to think in terms of priorities and keep an eye on the big picture.

Step 2. Assessing the validity of your task

To ensure the task is something you actually need to do, ask yourself the following questions:

- Do I really need to do this task?
- Is right now the best time? What would happen if I delay it for a week? A month? Forever?
- Do I need to do this task, or am I doing it because it

makes me feel good? In short, am I working on this task to escape from what I really should be doing?

There is nothing more unproductive than doing something you didn't need to do in the first place. Answering these questions can help you avoid making such a mistake.

Step 3. Clarifying what needs to be done

Before working on a task, be certain you know exactly what is required. Therefore, before starting any task, ask yourself:

• What exactly do I need to do here?

• What am I trying to accomplish?

• What does the finished product look like?

Be specific. By knowing exactly what the output needs to be, you'll be able to optimize your approach and tackle the task more effectively.

Step 4. Determining whether you should be the person doing it

You have strengths, but you also have weaknesses. Whenever possible, try to delegate any task someone else can do better, faster or more cheaply than you. Ask yourself the following questions:

- Is this task really worth my time?
- Can someone else do it better than me? If so, can I ask for help?
- What would happen if I simply remove/postpone this task?
- Do I enjoy working on this task? Does it motivate me?

Little by little, you want to get into the habit of outsourcing everything you're not good at and focus only on the high-value tasks at which you excel.

Step 5. Finding out the most effective way to tackle a task

Just taking a few minutes to work out the best way to approach a task can save you so much time. Ask yourself the following questions:

- What tool(s) can I use, people can I ask, or method can I rely on to complete this task as efficiently and effectively as possible?
- What skill(s) could I learn or improve to help me complete this task faster in the future?

Step 6. Batching the task with other similar tasks

Some jobs can be combined with other tasks that require the same type of effort or preparation. For instance, many YouTubers block one full day a week to record videos, as opposed to creating one video every day.

Ask yourself:

- Can I batch this task with other similar tasks to boost my productivity?

Step 7. Automating/systemizing your task

Finally, you want to find ways to automate or systemize your task, especially if it's a repetitive one. Ask yourself:

- Can I create templates to reuse every time I work on this, or on similar tasks? For instance, you could design templates for the specific emails, presentations or documents you need to create over and over.
- Can I create a checklist? Checklists provide you with

specific steps to follow, making it less likely you will become distracted or confused.

By following this seven-step approach you can boost your productivity significantly. Even though it may take time for you to internalize this process, once you do, it will become almost automatic.

Part III. Empower your model of reality

1. Design an empowering environment

A. Changing your peer group

Answer the following questions:

Who do I want to spend more time with?

Who do I want to spend less time with?

Who are the people who have already achieved the goals I seek to achieve?

Where can I find these positive and supportive people?

1) How to protect yourself from negative people

Make a list of all the people who are having a negative impact on your life:

-

-

-

-

-

-

Answer the following question: How likely am I to achieve my goal if I hang out with the same people?

2) Surround yourself with people who will support you

a. Join groups of like-minded people

What group or groups could you join? Who could you contact?

b. Create your own event

Who do you want to attract into your life, and what kind of event could you organize that would appeal to them?

c. Look for a mentor/d. Hire a coach

If necessary, start looking for people who could mentor you or coach you.

B. Change your physical environment

What one thing could you do to spend more time with people who will support your goal?

What one thing could you do to create a more positive environment to motivate you to work on your goal?

What one thing could you do to optimize your current environment and make it easier to work on your goal?

C. Optimizing your digital environment

Optimize your digital environment by:

- Turning off phone notifications
- Checking your emails as few times as possible, (if possible, limit your email access to once or twice per day)

- Turning off WIFI or stay away from social media or any other sources of online distraction, (e.g. install software to remove distractions as and when necessary)
- Unsubscribing from newsletters

2. Developing unshakeable confidence

A. Understanding belief

Remember the following when it comes to cultivating belief:

1. Not possible —> 2. possible —> 3. probable —> 4. inevitable

B. Adopting key empowering beliefs

Print out the page with the five beliefs at the end of this action guide and read them on a regular basis. Think of them often. If you identify other great beliefs you want to adopt, add them to your repertory. As a reminder, the five beliefs are:

1. I can always improve over the long term
2. If someone else can, I can
3. If I can do it once, I can do it again
4. Others will give up, therefore, I will succeed
5. Success is inevitable

C. Achieving goals consistently

Complete the exercises below:

- Re-using the goal you've been working with, break it down into yearly, monthly, weekly and daily goals.
- For the next thirty days, set three simple daily tasks and make sure you complete them.

Your goal_____

Now, break it down.

Yearly goals:

-

-

-

Monthly goals:

-

-

-

Weekly goals:

-

-

-

Daily goals:

-

-

-

D. Conditioning your mind

1) Using affirmations

Create your own affirmations using the few tips to create your own affirmations:

- **State your affirmation in the present tense.**
- **Avoid using negatives** and state your affirmation in the positive form. For instance, say "I'm courageous" rather than "I'm no longer afraid."
- **Aim to change your physiological state.** Engage your body and experiment with different vocal tones. This will add power to your affirmation.
- **Use the power of visualization.** See yourself in specific situations that relate to your affirmation, then try to feel as though you already have what you want. Engaging your emotions this way will make your affirmation significantly more powerful.

Write down your own affirmations below:

-

-

-

-

2) Changing your self-talk

Write down a few sentences you can use as positive self-talk to overcome some of the limiting beliefs you hold relating to your goal.

Your limiting belief #1:

Your positive self-talk:

Your limiting belief #2:

Your positive self-talk:

Your limiting belief #3:

Your positive self-talk:

3) Practicing visualization

Spend a few minutes every morning visualizing yourself moving toward your goal and accomplishing it. Additionally, think about your goals throughout your day.

E. Cultivating self-compassion

Complete the exercises below:

- Undertake a seven-day self-compassion challenge.
- Whenever you notice you start beating yourself up, change your self-talk. Tell yourself you're doing okay. Encourage yourself. Be kind to yourself.

3. Expand your field of possibilities

A. Generating luck

1) Refusing to believe in luck

Answer the following question:

If there wasn't such thing as luck, what would you do differently to improve the chance you achieve your goal? Write down everything that comes to mind:

-

-

-

-

-

-

-

-

-

-

-

2) Repeatedly thinking about what you want

Spend a few minutes focusing on what you want every day. I recommend you focus on your goal twice (first thing in the morning and before going to bed).

3) Broadcasting your desires to the world

What is one specific thing you could do to broadcast your goals to people who could potentially help you achieve it?

4) Taking consistent action in line with a clearly defined strategy

Make sure you take consistent action toward your goal. These actions should be the ones you identified in 5. *How to create an effective process, B. Putting in place an effective process.*

5) Learning as much as you can from the feedback you receive from reality

Make sure you learn from every setback you face. Ask yourself, what's great about it? What can I learn from that situation?

B. Asking yourself empowering questions

Answer the questions below:

How can I achieve my goal? What can I do to help me reach it?

What if I could achieve my goal? What if it was possible?

C. Taking consistent action

1) The benefits of taking action

Answer the following questions:

How well is my current approach working for me?

Am I really taking enough action to reach my goal?

What would taking massive action mean to me?

2) Doubling down on what works

Answer the following questions:

What, if anything, is bringing me the best results?

What could I do to double down on that success?

D. Leveraging the power of gratitude

Practice one of the exercises below for at least fourteen days:

- Write down things you're grateful for.
- Thank people who crossed your life.
- Focus on one object and appreciate its existence.
- Listen to gratitude song/guided meditation.

5 Key Empowering Beliefs

1. I can always improve over the long term
2. If someone else can, I can
3. If I can do it once, I can do it again
4. Others will give up, therefore, I will succeed
5. Success is inevitable

Printed in Great Britain
by Amazon